REASONING SKILLS FOR LAW ENFORCEMENT EXAMS

Other Titles of Interest from LearningExpress

Math Skills for Law Enforcement Exams

REASONING SKILLS FOR LAW ENFORCEMENT EXAMS

LEARNINGEXPRESS®

NEW YORK

Copyright © 2010 Learning Express, LLC.

All rights reserved under International and Pan-American Copyright Conventions. Published in the United States by LearningExpress, LLC, New York.

Library of Congress Cataloging-in-Publication Data:
Reasoning for law enforcement.—1st ed.
    p. cm.
  ISBN 978-1-57685-723-6
  1. Law enforcement—Examinations.   2. Reasoning.   3. Problem solving.   I. LearningExpress
(Organization)
  HV7921.R39 2010
  363.2076—dc22

                                                                        2009036631

Printed in the United States of America

9 8 7 6 5 4 3 2 1

First Edition

ISBN-13: 978-1-57685-723-6

Regarding the Information in This Book
We attempt to verify the information presented in our books prior to publication. It is always a good idea, however, to double-check such important information as minimum requirements, application and testing procedures, and deadlines with your local law enforcement agency, as such information can change from time to time.

For more information or to place an order, contact LearningExpress at:
  2 Rector Street
  26th Floor
  New York, NY 10006

Or visit us at:
  www.learnatest.com

CONTRIBUTOR ▶

Christopher W. Ortiz, Ph.D., is a Sergeant with the Glen Cove (NY) Police Department. In addition to his work as a police officer, he is a Criminal Justice Lecturer at New York Institute of Technology. He holds a Ph.D. in Criminal Justice from John Jay College of Criminal Justice and has conducted multiple research projects in the area of policing for the Police Foundation, the Vera Institute of Justice, the Police Assessment Resource Center, and the Rand Corporation.

CONTENTS

CONTENTS

How to Use ▶ This Book

Congratulations! You have decided to pursue a career in law enforcement. As you will soon find for yourself, many people who have entered a career in law enforcement regard it as one of the best decisions that they have ever made. Now that your mind has been made up, it is time to begin working toward your ultimate goal—landing your dream career in law enforcement.

Introduction

The lessons contained in this book were designed to give you a competitive edge on a broad base of law enforcement entrance exams. As you will see, reasoning is one of the most widely tested skills on these exams. In fact, just about every law enforcement entrance exam will contain a section testing your reasoning or judgment ability. This holds true if you are testing to become a police officer, a federal agent, or a probation officer. Therefore, you will find this book to be an excellent asset as you begin to prepare for your exam and ultimately, your career.

Why Study Reasoning and Critical Thinking Skills?

Regardless of the law enforcement area you have chosen for your career, you'll have to make tough decisions on a regular basis. As you work your way through these decisions, you will find that you have to rely on reasoning, critical analysis, and problem-solving skills. Taken together, these skills form the basis of reasoning and critical thinking. For this reason you will find that reasoning and critical thinking skills will serve you well in your chosen law enforcement career. In fact, you will come to rely on reasoning skills greatly as these skills form the basis for your actions and reactions while on the job. How do you know what is the appropriate action to take at the scene of a crime? How do you resolve a dispute between two people who believe that their version of a situation is the correct version? How do you evaluate evidence and take action based upon your assessment? The answer to all these, and indeed a great many more questions, is through the use of reasoning and critical thinking skills. These skills provide you with a pathway for discerning the truth and taking action based upon evidence.

There is a second and more immediate need to study reasoning and critical thinking, and that is the fact that nearly all law enforcement entrance exams will have a section testing these skills. Some exams may even devote nearly half of all questions to testing your reasoning abilities. The reason for this should be obvious by this point: In order to have a successful law enforcement career, candidates must possess superior critical thinking, logical reasoning, and problem-solving skills. Although it may sound like a tough requirement, the reality is that the skill set needed to master these various areas are really one and the same: Reasoning skills. With this in mind, let's take a look at how reasoning skills are assessed on various law enforcement entrance exams.

Reasoning Skills and Law Enforcement Exams

The structure of the reasoning skills section on law enforcement exams are as varied as the jobs themselves. The reason for this is that each career develops its own entrance exam and sets its own priorities in regard to the standards candidates will possess. Therefore, the police officer exam may contain more critical thinking/logical reasoning questions than the corrections officer exam and less than the federal agent exam. In addition to this, each exam has a different name for the critical thinking/logical reasoning section. What is important for you to remember is that whether the section is called "Logical Reasoning," "Situational Judgment," or simply "Problem Solving," the skills needed to think through these questions and arrive at the correct answer are all the same. Take a look at the following list:

- **Reasoning:** a sufficient ground of explanation or of logical defense; something that supports a conclusion or explains a fact.
- **Decision Making:** the act or process of deciding; a determination arrived at after consideration; a conclusion
- **Problem-Solving Skills:** the process of overcoming difficulties or obstacles encountered in the attainment of a goal or objective; the process of resolving problems
- **Judgment:** the process of forming an opinion or evaluation by discerning and comparing.
- **Logical Reasoning:** The process of using a rational, systematic series of steps based on sound reasoning to arrive at a conclusion

The preceding list defines the words or concepts that are used to describe the reasoning skills sections on various law enforcement exams. Notice that all the definitions have the same basic skills and processes involved: explanation, evaluation, decision, and conclusion. In essence, although each item in the previous list has a slightly different definition, they are all extremely similar in nature. When brought down to the least common denominator, all of these varied processes really boil down to the ability to analyze a problem and formulate a good decision based upon the evidence and facts given to you. Take a look at this next list:

CAREER	REASONING SKILL SECTION
Deputy Sheriff	Judgment
Federal Agent	Verbal Reasoning
Police Officer	Judgment
Police Sergeant	Judgment
Probation Officer	Concepts
Parole Officer	Concepts
State Police	Problem Solving
Treasury Agent	Investigative Concepts
Border Patrol	Logical Reasoning
Corrections Officer	Situational Reasoning

This list contains ten law enforcement careers. The careers are varied in function and job responsibilities and may even vary in terms of location in the governmental structure (federal vs. state). Next to each of these careers, you will see the exact name of the reasoning skills section on their respective entry exam. Again, notice that the reasoning skills sections have different names. Some call reasoning skills "problem solving" while others call it "investigative concepts." Regardless of the name, the skills involved to work through these sections of the exams are the same. Therefore, in deciding to work on your reasoning skills you have also unknowingly decided to boost you judgment, verbal reasoning, concepts, problem-solving, logical reasoning, and situational reasoning skills.

1 ▶ Critical Thinking and Reasoning Skills

LESSON SUMMARY
You've probably heard the terms "critical thinking" and "reasoning skills" many times, in many different contexts. But what exactly does it mean to think critically? And just what are reasoning skills? This lesson will answer these questions and show you why critical thinking and reasoning skills are so important.

We all make decisions on a daily basis. Without the ability to make decisions, and more importantly, sound decisions, we would surely suffer embarrassment and possible injury on a continuous basis. But not all decisions are the same. Deciding what shirt to wear on a particular day is a very different decision than deciding whether to use deadly physical force against a suspected burglar. Both have some level of importance, but the consequences of wearing the wrong shirt pale in comparison to the unwarranted shooting of an unarmed burglary suspect. This is just one example of the type of decisions that law enforcement officers are trusted to make each day, decisions that clearly demonstrate why critical thinking skills are an important component for a law enforcement candidate to possess.

Regardless of the law enforcement area you have chosen for your career, you'll have to make tough decisions on a regular basis. This fact has not been lost on those who create law enforcement entrance exams. Regardless of the specific job task (corrections, policing, customs, etc.), entrance exams for these careers all contain lengthy sections testing critical thinking and logical reasoning skills. The reason for this is clear. Simply stated, these careers require people who can think through complicated problems on a moment's notice and arrive at a good sound legal course of action. While there's no guarantee you'll be hired based on the first law enforcement entrance exam you take, there is a way to significantly improve your odds—and that is by improving your critical thinking and reasoning skills. This book and the lessons it contains will assist you in doing just that.

What Are Critical Thinking and Reasoning Skills?

Perhaps the most common problem facing law enforcement candidates is test anxiety. If you have registered for a civil service law enforcement officer exam, you may have already experienced some anxiety while reviewing the provided exam structure. Mixed into the sections that you may be most comfortable with, such as reading comprehension or map reading, you may have spotted a section titled "Critical Thinking" or "Logical Reasoning" and the anxiety set in. Do not worry! The reality is that you are just as familiar with critical thinking as you are with reading comprehension. Remember, you utilize critical thinking skills every day. Let's take a moment to define these terms more thoroughly so that you recognize what each is and then we can focus on how to improve them.

Critical Thinking

Think for a minute about the words *critical thinking*. What does this phrase mean? Essentially, **critical thinking** is a decision-making process. Specifically, critical thinking means carefully considering a problem, claim, question, or situation in order to determine the best solution. That is, when you think critically, you take the time to consider all sides of an issue, evaluate evidence, and imagine different scenarios and possible outcomes. Law enforcement offi-

cers perform this task multiple times each day almost without conscious thought. It sounds like a lot of work, but the same basic critical thinking skills can be applied to all types of law enforcement situations ranging from simple disputes to detailed homicide investigations.

Critical thinking is so important because it helps you determine:

- how to best solve a citizen's problem
- whether to accept or reject a suspect's claim
- how to best answer a superior's question
- how to best handle a conflict situation

Reasoning Skills

Reasoning skills, on the other hand, deal more with the process of getting from point A (the problem) to point B (the solution). For most decisions, the process of getting from A to B can be haphazard, as the consequences of your actions are not too significant. For important decisions, you will probably want to rely on sound reasoning. For law enforcement officers, the only acceptable way to get from point A to point B is through reason.

A **reason** is a motive or cause for something—a justification for thoughts, actions, or opinions. In other words, it's *why* you do, say, or think what you do. But your reasons for doing things aren't always reasonable—as you know if you've ever done or said something in the heat of the moment. **Reasoning skills** ask you to use good sense and base your reasons on facts, evidence, or logical conclusions rather than on your emotions. In law enforcement, you will often hear this difference described as *a mistake of the head versus a mistake of the heart*. Head mistakes can be solved through training. Heart mistakes are more difficult to solve because the person's motivations are not in line with the organization. In short, when you decide on the best way to handle a situation or determine the best solution to a problem, you should have *logical* (rather than purely *emotional*) reasons for coming to that conclusion. This is especially the case in law enforcement, which theoretically should be devoid of any emotional action.

> **Logical:** according to reason; according to conclusions drawn from evidence or good common sense
>
> **Emotional:** drawn from emotions, from intense mental feelings

The Role of Emotion in Law Enforcement

Is it possible to act without emotion? Is it possible for a person to take action without any physical or psychological feeling or reaction? Indeed it is possible, but those who do this are often diagnosed as sociopaths. In other words, stable, healthy human beings have emotions and cannot take action without some engagement of these feelings. When it is said that law enforcement officers must act based on the clear guidelines presented in the law, it does not mean they must be uncaring robots. What it means is that they must sometimes take action in spite of their emotions. They must choose to act based on laws and policies rather than their internal feelings. Does this mean that law enforcement officers never act based on emotion? No. It's perfectly valid to take your emotions into consideration when you make decisions. In fact, in most good decisions, emotion and reason are aligned within the same action. But if there's *no* logic or reason behind your decisions, you're usually in for trouble. Let's look at an example. You are a sheriff working the downtown area on night watch. The downtown area is a well-known drug hotspot. You observe two males engaged in a possible drug transaction. When you approach them, you recognize one as a drug dealer you have arrested numerous times before. You grab him, pat him down for weapons, and he allows you to search him for drugs, but you find nothing. You clearly saw them engaged in a drug

transaction, but somehow they were able to stash the drugs. What action should you take? In order to decide what to do, you first need to think critically. You'll want to be sure that you:

- carefully consider your options (arrest versus no arrest)
- consider different possibilities and outcomes of these actions
- have logical reasons to support your final decision, especially if you are going to make an arrest

Emotionally, you know this guy was dealing drugs and deserves to go to jail. Logically and reasonably, you do not have the level of evidence needed to support an arrest. Clearly, you must choose logic over emotion in this situation. In this instance, logic and reason relate directly to *probable cause*—the standard of evidence required for law enforcement officers to physically arrest a person suspected of committing a crime. You do not have the necessary evidence needed to support an arrest. Logically, you cannot come to the conclusion that this guy was selling drugs when you lack the evidence to support that conclusion.

Practice

1. Imagine that you are working in a prison as a corrections officer and you need to identify rival gang members so that you can keep them away from each other in the prison yard. You want to make sure that you identify all gang members, but you do not want to include any non-gang members. Apply critical thinking and reasoning skills to complete this job assignment. First, critical thinking: What different things should you take into consideration when deciding how to identify gang members? List at least five different considerations. Two are already listed for you.

Things to consider

1. They admit to being in a gang.
2. Other prisoners tell you they are in a gang.
3.
4.
5.

Answers

You probably listed several important identifiers, such as:

- clothing
- tattoos
- associates/friends
- jewelry/ accessories
- language
- use of gang signs/signals
- what neighborhood/city they lived in

Justifying Your Decision

One way to help ensure that you're using your critical thinking and reasoning skills is to always justify your decisions and actions. In law enforcement, justification is crucial. When an officer uses deadly physical force against a suspect the first question that is always asked is whether the shooting was justified. Why did the officer draw his weapon? Why did he decide to fire a shot? Was that the only possible solution? Justification is the reason for action. If the action was logical and reasonable, then the requirements for justification are usually met. If the reason was purely emotional and not based on the logic of evidence, then justification is not supported. As a law enforcement officer, all your decisions must be justified.

You may find it helpful to practice justifying everyday decisions and actions you make. You'll get to know your current decision-making process, and you'll be able to determine where in that process you can become more effective.

2. You are a police officer working the night watch. A call comes over the radio about an armed robbery that just occurred a block away from where you are. The suspect is described as being a white male, 6′4″, 250 pounds, wearing a red sweatshirt/blue jeans/Yankees baseball cap. He is armed with a silver handgun. You see a person running past you who matches this description exactly and you start to chase him. He suddenly turns toward you, lifts his arm, and points something at you. You draw your firearm and fire a shot. Are you justified? Using your critical thinking and reasoning skills, answer this question and support it with reasons for your choice. You can make up the specifics; what's important is that you include several different reasons that show you've thought about your decision carefully and critically.

Were you justified? Yes/No

Reasons for this choice:

_____

_____

_____

_____

_____

Answer

Answers will vary slightly here, but you should have some variation of the following answer.

Were you justified? *Yes*

Reasons for this choice
- He matched the description of the armed robber exactly.
- The robbery occurred down the block.
- The robbery just happened.
- He was running from the location of the robbery.
- He turned toward me in a threatening manner.
- He raised his hand as if he was about to shoot me.
- Based on all these facts, I reasonably thought that he was the robber and that he was armed with a gun that he was about to use to shoot me.

Why Critical Thinking and Reasoning Skills Are Important

As the previous exercise illustrates, critical thinking and logical reasoning skills are important for law enforcement candidates and officers to possess. In fact, many of the basic legal requirements for law enforcement officers are grounded on the basic foundations of logic and reasonableness. In deciding whether a police officer's actions were justified, the court does not seek to determine whether the officer was right or wrong, they just want to ensure that the officer's actions were reasonable given the circumstances.

In your career, you will come to rely on reasoning skills greatly. But, for your purposes at this point, you will need to develop these skills so that you can take that first step toward becoming a law enforcement officer by performing well on the written entrance examination. In addition, you will face (if you don't already) situations on the job, at home, and at school that require critical thinking and reasoning skills. By improving these skills, you can improve your success in everything you do. Specifically, strong critical thinking and reasoning skills will help you:

- compose and support strong, logical arguments
- assess the validity of other people's arguments
- make more effective and logical decisions
- solve problems more efficiently

Essentially, these four skills make up problem-solving skills. For example, if someone wants to change your mind and convince you of something, you have a problem—you have to decide whether to change your beliefs, whether to accept that person's argument. Similarly, when you have a choice to make, or a position you'd like to support, you have a different type of problem to solve—what choice to make, how to support your position. Thus, this book will use the term *problem solving* to refer to any one of these situations. **Problem solving** is the focus of the next lesson.

In Short

Critical thinking is the act of carefully considering a problem, claim, question, or situation in order to determine the best solution. Reasoning skills, which go hand-in-hand with critical thinking, ask you to base your decisions on facts, evidence, or logical conclusions. Critical thinking and reasoning skills are implemented simultaneously to help you make smarter decisions and solve problems effectively. They also help you make stronger arguments and better evaluate the arguments of others. Taken together, these skills will become invaluable to you over the course of your law enforcement career.

Notice how many decisions you make throughout the day and how many different problems you face. What kind of decisions and problems do you encounter most often at home? At work? At school?

SKILL BUILDING UNTIL NEXT TIME

- Write down the process you went through to make a decision or solve a problem today. What did you do to get from point A, the problem, to point B, the solution?
- Evaluate a decision or problem you solved recently. Do you think it was a wise decision or effective solution? Why or why not? Did you consider the range of issues, or did you neglect to take certain issues into consideration? Did you make your decision based mostly on reason or mostly on your emotions?

2 ▶ Problem-Solving Strategies

LESSON SUMMARY

You face problems every day, and sometimes they can be overwhelming. In this lesson, you'll learn how to pinpoint the main issue of a problem and how to break it down into its various parts, thus making the problem more manageable.

Problem solving has become the new maxim in law enforcement. For years, law enforcement agencies have emphasized a need to address the root causes of crime and social problems rather than just responding to their outcomes. For this reason, problem-solving skills have emerged as a testable component on many law enforcement entrance exams and for good reason. The majority of situations that you will find yourself in as a law enforcement officer can be viewed through a problem-solving approach. For instance, a corrections officer deciding how to defuse prisoner tension, a border patrol agent deciding how to best cover hundreds of miles of open boarder, or a police officer deciding whether to use deadly physical force. Luckily, not all situations or problems are as formidable as these. But all law enforcement officers face their share of problems, and it's important to handle them quickly and effectively. Critical thinking and reasoning skills can help you do just that.

Definition: What Is a Problem?

Let's begin by defining the word *problem*. In terms of critical thinking and reasoning skills, a problem is any situation or matter that is challenging to solve, thus requiring you to make a difficult decision. That decision can be about anything—how to solve a homicide, how to handle a prisoner hostage situation, how to convince a complainant to see your point of view, or even how to solve a major crime spree. In terms of law enforcement, almost any situation that you are called to respond to constitutes a problem and it is your job to solve it. The following steps will help you to become an excellent problem solver.

Identify the Problem

The first step to solving any problem is to *identify the problem*. This may sound obvious—of course you need to know what the problem is. But it's important to take this step, because in real life, with all its complications, it's easy to lose sight of the real problem at hand. When this happens, the problem becomes much more complicated than it needs to be because you end up focusing on secondary issues rather than what's really at stake. Once you've identified the problem, you need to break it down into its parts. This is an essential step because it gives you a sense of the scope of the problem. How big is it? How many issues are there? Sometimes, at first glance, problems seem so big that a solution seems impossible. Other times, you may underestimate the size of a problem and end up making a poor decision because you overlook an important factor. By breaking a problem down into its parts, you may find it's not as big a problem as you thought—or that it's much more complicated than you initially anticipated.

Either way, when you break a problem down, you make it manageable—big or small, you can take it on one issue at a time.

Practice

To see exactly how breaking down a problem works, read the following scenario:

> You are a probation officer with a caseload of 42 probationers. Your job is to monitor the probationers in order to ensure that they do not commit any other crimes. One of your probationers is having a difficult time finding a job. He has applied for several entry level jobs, but has not been offered employment at any. Without employment, he will no longer be able to afford his rent. In addition, he and his wife recently separated.

1. Which of the following best expresses the real issue or problem?
   a. finding the probationer employment
   b. finding the probationer a new apartment
   c. how to keep the probationer from committing any more crimes
   d. assisting the probationer with finding marriage counseling

Answer

The correct answer is choice **c**—how to keep the probationer from committing any more crimes. This is the main problem you must solve—the big picture. Notice, however, that each of the other answers above is a *sub*issue that should be addressed; each of the other options is a *specific* way to address the larger, more general problem. It's important to remember that choices **a**, **b**, and **d** are just *parts* of the problem. Also, there may be other parts that are not listed here. If one of those options doesn't work out, other viable options remain.

Practice

Here's another scenario:

> You are a corrections officer working medium security at a county jail. Two prisoners have had a serious fight. Numerous other prisoners witnessed the fight and everyone is agitated now. Several other small fights and altercations have broken out on the tier.

2. Which of the following best expresses the real issue or problem?
  a. who started the fight
  b. what really happened
  c. whose version of what happened you should believe
  d. how to restore peace to the tier
  e. how to prevent future disputes between these two

Answer

This situation is a bit more complicated than the first. To get the best answer, you need to ask yourself where the real issue lies, what's really at stake. Is it more important to determine what happened, or to fix the result of what happened? It's very easy to get caught up in the details of the fight, trying to find out who's to blame. But while that's important, the real problem is to figure out how to keep peace in the tier, which is reflected in choice **d**. The other choices illustrate different components of that larger problem. In order to solve this problem, you *do* need to address both issues in choices **a** and **b**: who started it and what really happened. And in order to do that, you'll need to take into consideration choice **c** as well—whose version of what happened you should believe. Furthermore, you should also keep choice **e** in mind so that you can minimize this type of problem in the future.

Breaking the Problem into Its Parts

Now that you've identified the main problem, it's time to identify the various parts of that problem. You already know several issues.

Problem: How to restore peace to the tier

Parts of the problem
- who started the fight
- what really happened
- whose version of what happened you should believe
- how to prevent future disputes

Practice

3. Each of these issues must be addressed in order to solve the problem. But these aren't the only issues. Can you think of any other parts of this problem? Write them here:

_____

_____

_____

_____

_____

Answers

You might have added several issues, such as:

Parts of the problem
- who started the fight
- what really happened
- whose version of what happened you should believe

- how to prevent future disputes
- what punishment should be handed out
- how the other prisoners should be dealt with
- how to exercise your authority
- how to carry out your investigation
- If you thought of any other issues, add them here.

_____

_____

Prioritizing Issues

The next step is to decide how to tackle the issues just described. Clearly, some are more important than others, and some must be addressed before others. That's why it's essential to rank the parts of the problem in the order in which you think they should be addressed.

Which issues need to be dealt with first? Second? Third? Are there some issues that must be solved before you can deal with others?

Practice

4. Use your critical thinking and reasoning skills to prioritize the previously mentioned issues.

_____

_____

_____

_____

_____

_____

Answer

Answers will vary, depending upon what other issues you identified. Here's how the previous list might be prioritized.

Parts of the problem, in order of importance
- how to exercise your authority
- how to carry out your investigation
- who started the fight
- what really happened
- whose version of what happened you should believe
- how to punish the prisoners who were fighting
- how to prevent future fights on the tier

Relevance of Issues

When you're breaking down a problem, it's important that you make sure your issues are relevant to the problem. That is, each issue should be clearly related to the matter at hand. It's often obvious when something isn't relevant. Whether you like your pizza plain or with pepperoni, for example, clearly has nothing to do with this problem. But something like which prisoner has a known gang affiliation might. It depends on what the fight was about. In any attempt at solving problems, relevance of issues must be taken into account.

Practice

Read the following scenario carefully and then answer the questions that follow.

You are a police officer in the City of Oz. A home was burglarized in the northeast section of town. Upon arrival you are met by the homeowner. He states that a large sum of cash was taken from a safe. As you interview him, he begins to tell you about a possible drug house at the end of the block. Numerous people go in and out of the home at all hours of the night. He also tells you about a neighbor who was just released from prison. He believes that he is back to his old criminal ways. Finally, he tells you about a large group of kids who make noise all night long and he wants to know what you plan on doing about it.

5. The main problem or issue is
    a. how to deal with the noisy kids.
    b. solving the burglary.
    c. how to deal with the possible drug house.
    d. whether the neighbor is committing crimes again.

6. What are the parts of the problem?
    ■ _____
    ■ _____
    ■ _____
    ■ _____
    ■ _____

7. In what order should you address the parts of the problem?
    a. _____
    b. _____
    c. _____
    d. _____
    e. _____

Answers

5. The main problem is choice **b**, solving the burglary.

6. You may have broken the problem down into the following parts:
    ■ How did the burglar enter the home?
    ■ How can we close down the drug house?
    ■ How did the burglar open the safe?
    ■ How can we stop the kids from making noise?
    ■ How did the burglar know about the money?
    ■ Does the drug house have anything to do with the burglary?
    ■ Does the neighbor have anything to do with the burglary?

7. You should probably address the parts of the problem in the following order:
    1. How did the burglar enter the home?
    2. How did the burglar open the safe?
    3. How did the burglar know about the money?
    4. How do I deal with the drug house?
    5. Does the drug house have anything to do with the burglary?
    6. Does the neighbor have anything to do with the burglary?

In Short

A **problem** is any situation or matter that is challenging to solve, thus requiring you to make a difficult decision. Breaking problems down can help you make even big problems manageable. The first step to effective problem solving is to clearly identify the main problem. Then, break the problem down into its various parts. After you rank the parts in order of priority, check to make sure each issue is relevant. As a law enforcement officer, this entire process will become second nature to you and you will find yourself walking through these steps subconsciously.

SKILL BUILDING UNTIL NEXT TIME

- Take a problem that you come across today and break it down. Identify the main issue and each of its parts. Then, prioritize the parts.
- While sitcoms often drastically simplify the problems we face in real life, dramas like *Law & Order* and *ER* often show characters dealing with complex problems. Watch one of these shows and notice how the characters work through their problems. Do they correctly identify the real problem? Do they break it down into its parts? Evaluate their problem-solving strategies.

Thinking versus Knowing

LESSON SUMMARY

One of the keys to effective critical thinking and reasoning skills is the ability to distinguish between fact and opinion. This lesson will show you the difference—and why it matters.

I f you've ever watched the popular TV series *CSI*, you know that the investigators on the show rely heavily on *evidence* to prove their theories and solve their cases. What does this mean? It means that before they point any fingers, they use scientific proof to justify their claims. As a viewer, you may have an *opinion* as to who committed the crime in question—that is, you may *believe* one character over another. But according to the crime scene investigators, who did what and when is a matter of *fact*. That is, with enough evidence, they don't believe—they know because they can *prove* it. Law enforcement officers do not act based upon opinion, they act based upon fact.

Definition: Fact versus Opinion

Before we go any further, let's define *fact* and *opinion*.

Facts Are

- things *known* for certain to have happened
- things *known* for certain to be true
- things *known* for certain to exist

Opinions, on the other hand, are:

- things *believed* to have happened
- things *believed* to be true
- things *believed* to exist

Essentially, the difference between fact and opinion is the difference between *believing* and *knowing*. Opinions may be *based* on facts, but they are still what we *think*, not what we *know*. Opinions are debatable; facts usually are not. A good test for whether something is a fact or opinion is to ask yourself, "Can this statement be debated? Is this known for certain to be true?" If you can answer yes to the first question, you have an opinion; if you answer *yes* to the second, you have a fact. If you're not sure, then it's best to assume that it's an opinion until you can *verify* that it is indeed a fact.

Why the Difference between Fact and Opinion Is Important

When you're making decisions, it's important to be able to distinguish between fact and opinion—between what you or others *believe* and what you or others *know* to be true. When you make decisions, assess others' arguments, and support your own arguments, use facts, as they generally carry more weight than opinions. For example, if you are a police officer and you are testifying at a trial, you may not be totally convincing to a jury if you only give an opinion about a crime without the support of facts, but you will definitely be convincing if you back your opinions with facts. Furthermore, distinguishing between fact and opinion is important because people will often present their opinions as fact. When you're trying to make big decisions or solve complex problems, you need to know that you're working with evidence rather than emotions. Notice the difference between the following two examples:

> "I really think he murdered his wife. I don't think he liked her very much."
> "I really think he murdered his wife. His fingerprints were found on the murder weapon."

Notice in the second example, facts support the opinion that, "I really think he murdered his wife."

Practice

Read the following statements carefully. Which of the following are facts? Which are opinions? Write an **F** in the blank if the statement is a fact and an **O** if it is an opinion.

_____ **1.** Crimes are committed by drug addicts.

_____ **2.** Crime has fallen to historically low rates.

_____ **3.** Many criminals have addiction problems.

_____ **4.** Most criminals get off easy.

_____ **5.** Most crimes go unsolved.

Answers

1. O
2. F
3. F
4. O
5. F

Fact: based on what is **known**

Opinion: based on what is **believed**

Practice

To strengthen your ability to distinguish between fact and opinion, try turning a fact into an opinion. Here's a fact:

Americans pay federal, state, and local taxes.

An opinion is something debatable. Here are two opinions based on this fact:

Americans pay too much in taxes.
Americans should pay taxes only if they make over $40,000.

Now you try it.

6. **Fact:** Some states have raised their speed limits to 65 or more on major highways.

Opinion: _____

_____

_____

7. **Fact:** It is illegal to take another person's property.

Opinion: _____

_____

_____

8. **Fact:** Prison populations have reached their highest levels in the United States.

Opinion: _____

_____

_____

9. **Fact:** It is illegal to possess marijuana.

Opinion: _____

_____

_____

Answers

Answers will vary. Here are sample answers:
6. States that have raised their speed limits to over 65 are playing with fire.
7. Sometimes it's okay to take another person's property.
8. We don't send enough people to prison.
9. Marijuana is harmless.

Tentative Truths

Try this exercise. Label the following as either fact (**F**) or opinion (**O**).

_____ 10. I believe that the government has evidence of contact with aliens hidden in Roswell, New Mexico.

_____ 11. The government has evidence of contact with aliens hidden in Roswell, New Mexico.

You didn't by chance mark the first claim as **O** and the second claim as **F**, did you? If you did, it's easy to see why. The first claim is *presented* as an opinion ("I believe"), and it is therefore clearly an opinion. The second claim, however, is presented as a fact. But is it true? Is it something *known* for sure? Well, it can't really be proven or disproved, unless you have access to secret government documents. Statement 11 is what is called a **tentative truth**, since it is neither a fact nor an opinion. Until the truth of that matter can be verified—especially a matter that has been so controversial for so many years—it's best to hold on to a healthy measure of doubt.

Tentative truths need not deal with conspiracy theories or other issues of major importance. They can deal with issues as simple as this:

> The Toyota Corolla gets more than 30 miles per gallon.

This is a matter of fact, and it sounds like something that should be accepted as true, but unless you got in a Corolla and drove around, you may not be able to verify it. You can *tentatively* accept it as fact, especially if the source is credible. **Credibility** is the key determinant of whether you should accept facts you can't verify yourself. The next lesson shows you how to determine credibility.

Practice

Determine whether the following claims are facts (**F**), opinions (**O**), or claims that you should accept as tentative truths (**TT**):

12. Each state has laws against killing another person.

13. In New York State, homicide laws are found in the State Constitution.

14. There should be one law for the entire country covering homicide.

Answers

12. F
13. TT, unless you happen to know where the law is written in New York State, in which case you could call this a fact. In reality, this is a *false* fact; homicide laws in New York are found in the Penal Law.
14. O

Fact versus Opinion in Critical Reasoning

Now let's look at a situation where you have to use your critical thinking and reasoning skills to make a decision and where it will be important to distinguish between fact and opinion. In order to make a good decision, you need to know the difference between fact and opinion. You also have to be able to recognize when opinions are based on facts. First, let's continue to practice noticing the distinction between fact and opinion.

You are a police officer and you have been called to report to the scene of damaged property. You arrive at a house and notice that the front window is broken.

Practice

15. Read the following paragraph carefully. **Highlight** the facts and underline the opinions.

Careers in law enforcement are difficult to get. In order to even be considered, you must pass a written exam, take a physical, and possess good moral character. But a career in law enforcement can be exciting and rewarding in many ways. Currently, benefits and wages are comparable to those of many private-sector jobs and retirement benefits can even surpass those of some other careers. The effort to enter into a law enforcement career is well worth the time spent studying and preparing for the rigors of the hiring process.

Answers

How did you do? Was it easy to distinguish between fact and opinion? Here's what your marked-up passages should look like:

<u>Careers in law enforcement are difficult to get.</u> **In order to even be considered, you must pass a written exam, take a physical, and possess good moral character.** <u>But a career in law enforcement can be exciting and rewarding in many ways.</u> **Currently, benefits and wages are comparable to those of many private-sector jobs and retirement benefits can even surpass those of some other careers.** <u>The effort to enter into a law enforcement career is well worth the time spent studying and preparing for the rigors of the hiring process.</u>

In Short

Distinguishing between fact and opinion is vital to a career in law enforcement. To make wise decisions and solve problems effectively, you need to know the difference between what people *think* (opinion) and what people *know* (fact); between what people *believe* to be true (opinion) and what *has been proven* to be true (fact). You should also be able to determine whether something presented as fact is really true or if you should accept it as a tentative truth.

SKILL BUILDING UNTIL NEXT TIME

- Listen carefully to what people say today and try to determine whether they are stating a fact or expressing an opinion. If you're not sure, is it okay to accept it as a tentative truth?
- As you come across facts and opinions today, practice turning them into their opposites: Make facts out of opinions and opinions out of facts.

Who Makes the Claim?

LESSON SUMMARY

When we're faced with opinions and tentative truths, it's important to know how much we can trust our sources and how much they know about the subject at hand. This lesson will teach you how to evaluate the credibility of your sources so that you can make well-informed decisions.

Y ou are working your dream job as a police officer. It is your first week on patrol and you are excited and nervous at the same time. The dispatcher transmits over the radio and instructs you to respond to 132 Main Street for a neighbor dispute. As you arrive you see several people standing on the sidewalk arguing and yelling loudly at one another. Your academy training kicks in and you quickly identify the two main combatants, separate them, and begin to interview them in order to figure out what the problem is. You speak to Mr. Jones first. He tells you that he and his neighbor, Mr. Smith, were arguing over a parking space and that Mr. Smith punched him in the face. You then speak to Mr. Smith and he tells you the same thing, except he claims that Mr. Jones punched him in the face. You interview Mr. Smith's wife and she says that her husband was attacked and that he did nothing to provoke it. At the same time, Mr. Jones's nephew comes over and says he saw the entire incident and that Mr. Smith attacked his uncle because he parked in Mr. Smith's parking spot. So, how do you resolve this incident? Who should be arrested for battery? In this instance, you're faced with different versions of what occurred. Whose version of the events should you value the most here? How do you make your decision?

Definition: What Is Credibility?

When you're faced with a variety of opinions, one of the most important things to consider is the **credibility** of those giving their opinion. That is, you need to consider whose opinion is the most trustworthy and valid in the particular situation.

> Credibility: believability; trustworthiness

Credibility also plays a very important role when dealing with those tentative truths you encountered in the previous lesson. Whenever you're offered opinions or facts that you aren't comfortable accepting and aren't able to verify, the credibility of your source is crucial in helping you decide whether to accept these opinions or tentative truths.

How to Determine Credibility

Several factors determine the credibility of a source. One is your previous experience with that source. Do you have any reason to doubt the truthfulness or reliability of this source based on past experience? Next, you need to consider your source's potential for bias as well as level of expertise. But let's return to our opening scenario for a moment. In this situation, we have four different eyewitness versions to consider:

- what Mr. Smith claims happened
- what Mr. Jones claims happened
- what Mrs. Smith claims happened
- what Mr. Jones's nephew claims happened

Of the four, which is probably the *least* credible (least trustworthy) source, and why? In this scenario, they all have potential for bias. First and foremost, both Mr. Smith and Mr. Jones have an incentive to get you to believe their version of the events. The other two

witnesses also have potential for bias, as they are related to the two people involved in the argument. Because of this potential bias, you must be careful to rely on your observations and other evidence before you make your final conclusion. Let's examine bias

Recognizing Bias

A **bias** is an opinion or feeling that strongly favors one side over others; a predisposition to support one side; or a prejudice against other sides. Relatives of two combatants clearly have a large potential for bias in supporting their relative's version of events over that of others. In the prison setting, inmates belonging to the same gang may have allegiance to one another due to gang affiliation and may lie to protect each other. In this case, you should be suspect of accepting a fellow gang member's version of a fight between a person belonging to his gang and an outsider. It's important, therefore, to know as much as possible about your sources when deciding how heavily to weigh their opinions.

Practice

Read the following scenario. Write **B** next to anyone whom you think might be biased. If you think the person is likely to have an unbiased, reasonable opinion write **U** in the blank.

Scenario: A prisoner is suspected of selling drugs while in the prison yard. You interview the following people and review the following sources of evidence. Which person/source has the potential for bias and which are likely to be unbiased.

_____ **1.** The prisoner

_____ **2.** The prisoner's cell mate

_____ **3.** A corrections officer who witnessed a transaction

_____ **4.** Video from the yard

Answers

1. B
2. B
3. U
4. U

The prisoner (**1**) has a direct interest in having you believe that he is not selling drugs in the yard and may lie to avoid punishment. The cell mate (**2**) may also be biased and seek to protect his friend or may just be seeking to protect himself from being labeled a rat. A corrections officer is most likely to be unbiased, as he or she has taken an oath and is there to perform his or her duties. Video from the yard is the most unbiased source of information regarding the prisoner's drug activity.

Level of Expertise

Let's move on to another example. You are investigating a homicide. Mr. Jackson is lying on the floor of his apartment and appears to have been deceased for several hours. There are no gunshot wounds or any other apparent injuries. He appears to have just passed away with no struggle or fight. Mr. Jackson's daughter comes to the scene and says that she thinks that her father died of a heart attack. Another officer on-scene says that he believes he died of a stroke. Finally, the medical examiner arrives and says that Mr. Jackson committed suicide. Who should you believe? How do you determine whose opinion is most credible? It's not going to be easy, but let's provide some additional criteria for determining credibility. Once you identify any possible biases, you need to carefully consider the next criteria: **expertise**. Generally speaking, the more a person knows about a subject—the

more expertise he or she has in that area—the more comfortable you should feel accepting his or her opinion. That is, in general, the greater the expertise, the greater the credibility. In this situation, we have several levels of expertise; a layperson (the daughter), a person with prior experience (the police officer), and a medical doctor (the medical examiner).

Practice

Rank each of these three sources in each area of expertise. Use **1** for the source with the most expertise and **3** for the source with the least.

5. Knowledge of death investigations:
_____ daughter
_____ police officer
_____ medical examiner

Answers

5. Knowledge of death investigations: **1**, medical examiner; **2**, police officer; and **3**, daughter.

Clearly, the medical examiner holds the highest level of expertise in this situation. This may be followed by the police officer based upon his or her training and past experience. Finally, the daughter may be last, but she could be ranked higher if she also happens to be a nurse or a doctor.

Determining Level of Expertise

In many a courtroom, lawyers will call an expert witness to the stand to support their case. For example, in a murder case where the defendant is pleading insanity, the prosecution and the defense might call on psychologists who can provide expert opinions about the defendant's ability to distinguish between right and wrong. These expert witnesses are usually outside the case—that is, they are usually not involved in the alleged crime and usually do not have any relationship to or with the defendant; otherwise, they might be biased. For this testimony to be helpful to either side, however, the jury must be convinced that the expert witness is indeed an expert; they must be assured of his or her credibility. The lawyers will help establish the witness's credibility by pointing out one or more of the following credentials:

- education
- experience
- job or position
- reputation
- achievements

These five criteria are what you should examine when determining someone's level of expertise and, therefore, credibility. One category is not necessarily more important than the other, though generally a person's education and experience carry the most weight. An outstanding expert witness at this trial, therefore, might have the following profile:

Dr. Joanne Francis

Education: PhD, Harvard University
Experience: Ten years at County Medical Hospital; 15 years at Harvard Psychiatric Center
Position: Chief of Psychiatric Care at Harvard Psychiatric Center; teaches graduate courses at Harvard
Reputation: Ranked one of the ten best on the East Coast
Accomplishments: Has won several awards; was asked to serve on a federal judicial committee to establish guidelines for determining insanity; has written three textbooks and published 20 journal articles

Notice how strong Dr. Francis is in each of the five categories.

Special Case: Eyewitness Credibility

One of the most difficult but important times to determine credibility is when there are eyewitnesses to a crime or other incident. Unfortunately, just because someone was at the scene doesn't mean his or her account is credible. One obvious factor that can interfere with witness credibility is bias. Let's say two coworkers, Andrea and Brady, get in a fight. There are three witnesses. Al is Andrea's friend; Bea is Brady's friend; and Cecil is a friend of both Andrea and Brady. Chances are that what Al saw will favor Andrea and what Bea saw will favor Brady. What Cecil saw, however, will probably be closest to the unbiased truth.

Other factors can also interfere with witness credibility. If an incident occurs at a bar, for example, we have several possible interferences. It was probably dark, smoky, and noisy, and the witnesses may have been drinking, tired, or simply not paying very much attention to their surroundings. In all eyewitness accounts, the longer the time between the event and the time of questioning, the more unreliable the account of the witness will most likely be. Think for a minute about your childhood. Did you ever tell a story about something that happened when you were little, only to be corrected by a parent or sibling who says, "That's not what happened"? Their version is different. Why? Because our memory fades quickly and can be influenced by our own ideas about ourselves and others. Thus, there are at least four factors that influence the credibility of eyewitnesses:

1. bias
2. environment
3. physical and emotional condition of the witness
4. time between event and recollection of event

Practice

Imagine you are a police officer who has just arrived at the scene of a fight between two young men on a street corner. Three people witnessed the incident, which occurred at 9:00 P.M. You arrive and begin interviewing witnesses at 9:20 P.M. The street corner is well lit.

9. Who do you think is the most credible witness, and why?

   Witness A is an elderly woman who was sitting on the stoop about ten feet from the corner. She was wearing her glasses, but she admits that she needs a stronger prescription. Her hearing, however, is fine. She doesn't know either boy involved in the incident, though she's seen them around the neighborhood before.

   Witness B is a friend of one of the boys but does not know the other. He is an outstanding student at the local high school and a star basketball player. He was at the deli around the corner buying bread when he heard the boys shouting and came out to see what was going on. He had just had a fight with his girlfriend.

   Witness C is a stranger to the neighborhood. He was crossing the street toward the corner when the boys started fighting. He has 20/20 vision. He is 45 and has two teenage children. He was only a few feet away from the boys when the fight occurred.

Answer

9. Though **Witness C** may have been distracted by traffic, chances are he's the most credible eyewitness. He was heading toward the corner and was looking at the boys. He may not have been able to hear what happened in the beginning, but he should have been able to see exactly what occurred. His vision is perfect and there's no reason to suspect any bias.

   Witness A is probably next on the list. Although she may not have been able to see as clearly as **Witness C**, she was close enough to have heard what passed between the boys. Again, we have little reason to suspect bias. **Witness B** is probably the least credible witness.

   Although he has a good reputation, he has two strikes against him. The first is that he is friendly with one of the boys, so he may be biased. The second is that he had just had a fight with his girlfriend, so he may have been distracted and not paying much attention.

In Short

When you're making decisions and solving problems, it's important to consider the credibility of your sources. Law enforcement officers must become quick experts at recognizing bias and otherwise tainted testimony. To determine whether a source is trustworthy, you must first rule out the potential for bias and then evaluate the source's level of expertise. Expertise is determined by education, experience, job or position, reputation, and achievements. Eyewitness credibility, on the other hand, must take into consideration the witness's potential for bias, the environment, the condition of the witness, and the time lapse between the event and the witness's recollection of the event.

SKILL BUILDING UNTIL NEXT TIME

- As you talk to others today and hear any of their opinions or tentative truths, think about their credibility. What biases might they have, if any? What is their level of expertise? Remember, a source's credibility can change depending on the subject matter of the claim.
- Watch a detective or legal drama, like *CSI*, or *Law & Order*. As you watch, pay particular attention to how the detectives and lawyers determine the credibility of their witnesses and others involved in the case.

Partial Claims and Half-Truths

LESSON SUMMARY

Every day, we're bombarded with partial claims and half-truths aimed at getting us to buy a product or support a cause. This lesson shows you how to recognize incomplete claims and hidden agendas.

Law enforcement officers work in a world filled with half-truths. In the vast majority of cases that they are called upon to resolve, they will often be bombarded with biased stories being recounted by people with specific agendas. Often, these people will recount the facts of the incident in such a way as to be favorable to them by making partial claims and leaving out important parts of the story. Other people will only tell half-truths, omitting the parts that implicate them in the incident. A good law enforcement officer needs to see through these half-truths and get at a complete version of events. This is often achieved by weaving together several half-truths into a coherent fact-based story. The following is a typical 911 call:

911 Operator: *City Police Department. What's your emergency?*
Caller: I need the cops here at 99 Main Street.
911 Operator: *What's the emergency?*
Caller: I was walking down the street and this guy started yelling and punched me in the face. I need the cops here now.

911 Operator: I have units on the way, are you injured? Do you need medical attention?

Caller: I don't know. All I know is that I was walking down the street and this guy punched me.

As a patrol officer, you will be called on to respond to calls just like this. The caller will most likely insist that he was just minding his own business, walking down the street when he was attacked. In reality, the caller may have initiated the fight or instigated it in some other manner. Does this mean that he deserved to be punched? Maybe or maybe not. You will have to get beyond the half-truths by interviewing more people and getting additional renditions of the story. The following lesson will help you deal with these types of scenarios.

The Trouble with Incomplete Claims

Incomplete claims are just that, *incomplete*! Recall from earlier lessons that in order to think critically and effectively solve problems you first need to gather all the facts. Incomplete claims do not allow us to do this. They just present us with one version of the events in question, and this version can be far from factual. Let's look at a common example.

You're relaxing on your sofa watching your favorite television show when it's time for a commercial break. Suddenly, a handsome announcer comes on the screen and tells you that new Stain-Ex laundry detergent outperforms the leading brand *and* costs less! Sounds like a great product. But should you run out and buy it? Well, besides the fact that you're probably quite comfortable on your couch, the answer is no—at least not yet. Not until you investigate further. Why shouldn't you go out and buy Stain-Ex? After all, it "outperforms the leading brand" *and* "costs less!" So what's the problem? The problem is that while the announcer's claims *sound* like facts, they're really quite misleading—and meant to be. Maybe Stain-Ex did "outperform" the leading brand (which brand is that?), but in what category? Stain removing? Whitening? Brightening? Sudsing? Rinsing? Fragrance? The ad doesn't say. The claim *sounds* good, but because it is incomplete, you don't know exactly *what* it's claiming. And until you determine what it's claiming, it's difficult to accept it as even a tentative truth.

Practice

Here are several incomplete claims and comparisons. Rewrite them so that they're complete.

Example
Incomplete claim: Now with 20% more flavor!
Revised claim: Now with 20% more onion flavor than our old recipe!

1. **Incomplete claim:** Energy Batteries last longer!

   Revised claim:

   _____

   _____

2. **Incomplete claim:** New and improved Mildew-Gone is tougher.

   Revised claim:

   _____

   _____

3. **Incomplete claim:** Smooth-Touch toilet tissue—twice the paper at half the price!

   Revised claim:

   _____

   _____

Answers

Answers will vary. Here are some possible revisions:

1. Energy Batteries last two hours longer than Forever Last!
2. New and improved Mildew-Gone is tougher on mildew stains than our old formula.
3. Smooth-Touch toilet tissue—twice as much paper as Thompson tissue at half the price per roll!

Tests and Studies

The makers of the Stain-Ex commercial know you've become a savvy shopper, so they've remade their commercial. Now the announcer tells you: "Studies show that new Stain-Ex outperforms the leading brand in laboratory tests. And it costs less per fluid ounce than Tidy!" Clearly, they've fixed their "costs less" claim. But what about their tests? Can you now safely believe that Stain-Ex is a better detergent than the leading brand? Not necessarily. Again, what the ad says *sounds* great, but you have to remember that this is an ad, which means you have to question its credibility. Your questions should be all the more insistent because the ad doesn't tell you anything about the tests. You don't know, for example:

- Who conducted the studies?
- How were the studies conducted?
- What exactly was tested?
- What exactly were the results?

We'll spend a whole lesson talking about tests and studies later in the book. For now, however, it's important to remember that tests and studies can be manipulated to get specific results. In other words, it's important to have a healthy skepticism about tests, surveys, and studies. They should be accepted only as very tentative truths until you can find out the answers to the kind of questions asked above. I can say,

for example, that "four out of five dentists surveyed recommend CleanRight toothpaste to their patients." In order for this claim to be true, all I have to do is survey five dentists—four of whom are my friends and who I know *do* recommend that toothpaste. Is my survey impartial? Certainly not. But I can now make this claim, and it sounds good to the consumer. When analyzing studies, probably the most important thing to consider is who conducted the study. Why? Because knowing who conducts it can help determine whether it's legitimate. Do the conductors have anything at stake in the results? For example, if an independent consumer group conducted the Stain-Ex lab tests, would you feel better about accepting their claims as tentative truths? Absolutely; they're not very likely to be biased. But if the makers of Stain-Ex conducted the tests, the likelihood of bias is extremely high—you should be more skeptical about claims made by them. In the real world, it's often a little more complicated than this, but you get the idea; studies and surveys are not always to be trusted.

Practice

Read the following claims carefully. Write **C** for complete and credible and **I** for incomplete or incredible.

_____ **4.** Recent taste tests prove Rich Chocolate Frosting tastes best.

_____ **5.** According to a Temple University study, three out of five Philadelphia shoppers surveyed have used their debit cards instead of cash to pay for groceries at their local supermarkets.

_____ **6.** A recent survey shows Americans prefer Choco-Bites to regular chocolate chip cookies.

Answers

4. **I.** First, the validity of the taste tests should be questioned. Second, "tastes best" is a vague phrase.

5. **C.** This claim is credible—it's complete and precise. Also, because it's a university study of supermarkets, there's little chance for bias. Furthermore, the claim acknowledges that it's only three out of five shoppers *surveyed*. That is, they're not trying to suggest that they surveyed everyone.

6. **I.** This claim is problematic. First is the vagueness of the statement "a recent survey." Second, what exactly are "regular" chocolate chip cookies?

Averages

Recently, you heard someone on a talk show claim, "The average American teenager spends 29 hours per week watching television." What's wrong with this claim, other than the fact that it's a bit disturbing? The trouble with this claim lies in the word *average*— a word often misused, and often used to mislead. Here, the problem for the listener becomes *defining* "average." Who *is* the average American teenager? What age? What habits? What likes or dislikes? How we define "the average American teenager" can make a big difference in determining what this claim actually means. Sometimes, using the word *average* to describe something is good enough—like the *average banana*, for example. But often, average is in the eye of the beholder. My definition of an average teenager, for example, is probably quite different from my parents' definition, and both of our definitions are probably quite different from my 15-year-old cousin's idea of the average teen. The word *average* can also be troublesome when we're talking about numbers. Take, for example, the following advertisement.

Looking for a safe, secure place to start a family? Then come to Serenity, Virginia. With an average of ten acres per lot, our properties provide your children with plenty of space to grow and play. Our spacious lawns, tree-lined streets, and friendly neighbors make Serenity a great place to grow up!

Sounds like a terrific place, doesn't it? Unfortunately, this ad is very misleading if you think you're going to move onto a big property. In most cases, **average** means *mean*, the number reached by dividing the total number by the number of participants. Let's take a look at how Serenity came up with this number.

Here are the facts: In Serenity, there are 100 properties. Ten of those properties have 91 acres each. Ninety of those properties have only one acre each.

$$
\begin{array}{r}
10 \times 91 = 910 \\
90 \times 1 = \underline{90} \\
1,000 \text{ (total acres)} \\
\div \underline{100} \text{ (number of properties)} \\
10 \text{ (average acres per property)}
\end{array}
$$

Ten acres is the average, all right. But does that represent the majority? Does the average accurately suggest what most properties in Serenity are like? Obviously not. In Serenity, the typical house sits on just one acre, not ten. It's important to keep in mind that *average* does not necessarily mean *typical* or *usual*. Unfortunately, that's generally what people think of when they hear the word *average*. And that's why an ad like this can be so misleading.

Practice

Read the following claims carefully to determine whether the use of the word *average* is acceptable or problematic. If the word is problematic, explain why.

7. The average woman lives a happier life than the average man.

8. The average life span of American women is two years longer than that of Canadian women.

9. The average salary at Wyntex Corporation is $75,000.

Answers

7. Very problematic. Who is the "average" woman? The "average" man? Furthermore, how do you define "happier"? Happier in what way?
8. Acceptable.
9. Problematic. The salary range at a company like Wyntex can be so large that $75,000 may not represent the typical salary. If the president and CEO make $2 billion a year, for example, that clearly inflates the average. Meanwhile, most employees at the company may be making less than $40,000.

In Short

Half-truths and incomplete claims are the reality of law enforcement. Often, they can sound convincing but further investigation and fact finding is needed before any action can be taken. In other words, a critical thinker like you has to be wary of such claims. When people are trying to sway your opinion in their favor—as advertisers do hundreds of times each day, for instance—watch out for misleading claims and half-truths that make their cases sound stronger than they really are.

SKILL BUILDING UNTIL NEXT TIME

- Pick up a popular magazine and look for ads that make incomplete claims. Compare them to ads that show more respect for your judgment and give you more information.
- Listen carefully to others today at work, on the radio, or on television. Do you hear any incomplete claims? Do you notice any suspicious averages?

What's in a Word?

LESSON SUMMARY

The words people use can have a powerful effect on their listeners. By choosing certain words instead of others or by phrasing questions in a way that is meant to elicit a specific response, people may try to influence your thoughts or actions. This lesson shows you how to recognize this kind of subtle persuasion.

Your cousin likes to skydive, climb mountains, and race cars. How would you describe him?

- reckless
- adventurous
- free-spirited

As different as these words are, each one can be used to describe someone who engages in your cousin's activities. The word you choose, however, depends upon your opinion of these activities. Clearly, *free-spirited* is the word with the most positive slant; *adventurous* is more or less neutral; and *reckless* is negative. Your word choice will convey a particular image of your cousin whether you intend it to or not. Words are powerful, and they can influence us without us even realizing it. That's because they carry at least two layers of meaning: denotation and connotation. **Denotation** is a word's exact or dictionary meaning. **Connotation** is the implied or suggested meaning, the emotional impact that the word carries. For example, *thin*, *slender*, and *lean* all mean essentially the same thing—their denotation is the same—but they have different connotations. *Slender* suggests a gracefulness that *thin* and *lean* do not. *Lean*, on the other hand, suggests a hardness or scarcity that *thin* and *slender* do not.

Because words carry so much weight, advertisers, politicians, and anyone else who wants to convince you to believe one thing or another choose their words carefully. By using subtle persuasion techniques, they can often manipulate feelings and influence reactions so that viewers and listeners don't realize they're being swayed. The best way to prevent this kind of influence is to be aware of these techniques. If you can recognize them, they lose their power. It's like watching a magician on stage once you already know the secret behind his tricks. You appreciate his art, but you're no longer under his spell. There are three different subtle persuasion techniques we'll discuss in this lesson: *euphemisms*, *dysphemisms*, and *biased questions*.

Euphemisms and Dysphemisms

Euphemisms are the most common of the subtle persuasion techniques. You've probably even used them yourself many times without even realizing it. A euphemism is when a phrase—usually one that's harsh, negative, or offensive—is replaced with a milder or more positive expression. For example, there are many ways to say that someone has died. *Die* itself is a neutral word—it expresses the fact of death straightforwardly without any real *mood* attached to it. However, this word is often softened by replacing it with a euphemism, such as one of the following:

- passed away
- passed on
- is no longer with us
- expired
- departed
- deceased

Just as we can say *died* in a softer or more positive way—a way that suggests movement to a better place, for example—we can also say it in a cruder or more negative way, like one of the following:

- croaked
- kicked the bucket
- bit the dust

When we replace a positive or neutral expression with one that is negative or unpleasant, we're using a **dysphemism**. Euphemisms and dysphemisms are used more than ever these days, especially in advertising, the media, and by politicians to influence our thoughts and feelings. Take, for example, the phrase *used cars*. Used car dealers used to sell *used cars*—now they sell *previously owned vehicles*. See the euphemism? The more pleasant phrase *previously owned* doesn't carry the suggestion of someone else *using*—just *owning*. Euphemisms are used a great deal in political and social issues. If you oppose abortion, for example, then you are *pro-life*. If you support the right to abort, on the other hand, you're *pro-choice*. See how important these euphemisms are? How could someone be *against* life? *Against* choice?

Euphemism: a milder or more positive expression used to replace a negative or unpleasant one

Dysphemism: a negative or unpleasant expression used to replace a neutral or positive one

Denotation: the dictionary meaning of a word

Connotation: the emotional impact or implied meaning of a word

Practice

Read each of the following words or phrases and write a euphemism and dysphemism for each.

1. medical practitioner

2. odor

3. geriatric

Answers

There are many possible answers. Here are a few:

Euphemism	Dysphemism
1. healer	butcher
2. fragrance	stench
3. elderly	ancient

Practice

Read sentences 4 through 7 carefully. If you notice a euphemism, write an **E** in the blank. If you notice a dysphemism, write a **D**. If the sentence is neutral, write **N**.

_____ **4.** Al saved a lot of money on his taxes this year with his creative accounting techniques.

_____ **5.** She is very good at taking care of details.

_____ **6.** He's not crazy; he's just a little unusual, that's all.

_____ **7.** I'm off to see my shrink.

Answers

4. E, "creative accounting techniques"
5. N
6. E, "a little unusual"
7. D, "shrink"

Biased Questions

Imagine someone stops you on the street and asks you to participate in a survey about tax cuts. You agree, and she asks you the following questions:

Do you support tax cuts that benefit only the wealthy and neglect the needs of those with low incomes?

Do you think the government should be allowed to make tax cuts that exclude the poor and uneducated?

No matter how you feel about tax cuts, chances are you can't answer anything but *no* to these questions. Why? Because if you say *yes*, it sounds like you are not empathetic to the needs of those who are helpless. These questions are phrased unfairly, making it difficult for you to give a fair answer. In other words, inherent in the questions is a certain attitude toward tax cuts—in this case, a negative one—that *prejudices* the questions. In short, the questions aren't fair—they're biased. Notice how these particular questions use dysphemisms to bias the questions and pressure you to answer them a certain way. In this example, *tax cuts* becomes equivalent to negative terms such as *neglect* and *exclude*.

EXAMPLES OF EUPHEMISMS AND DYSPHEMISMS		
WORD OR PHRASE	**EUPHEMISM**	**DYSPHEMISM**
fan	aficionado	zealot
inexpensive	economical	cheap
grandstander	public servant	lackey
old maid	bachelorette	spinster

Here is how euphemisms might be used to bias the questions toward the opposing point of view:

> Do you support tax cuts that will benefit all socioeconomic levels of society and help improve the economy?

> Do you think the government should be allowed to make tax cuts that give people's hard-earned money back to them?

This time, notice how saying *yes* is much easier than saying *no*. If you say *no* to the first question, it sounds like you are indifferent to what happens to you and your society. If you say *no* to the second question, it sounds like you are without compassion and don't believe that people deserve to keep what they earn. Here are the questions revised once again so that you can answer *yes* or *no* fairly:

> Do you support tax cuts?

> Do you think the government should be allowed to decide when to make tax cuts?

Professional surveys will be careful to ask fair questions, but when political organizations, advertisers, and other groups or individuals have an agenda, they may use biased questions to elicit specific results. Similarly, anyone who wants to influence you may use biased questions to get you to respond in a certain way. That's why it's important for you to recognize when a question is fair and when it's biased.

Practice

Read the following questions carefully. If you think the question is biased, write a **B** in the blank. If you think it's unbiased, write a **U**.

_____ **8.** What did you think of that lousy movie?

_____ **9.** Do you think the driving age should be raised to 18?

_____ **10.** Are you going to vote to reelect that crooked politician for governor?

_____ **11.** Do you support the destruction of rain forests rich in natural resources so that wealthy companies can flourish?

_____ **12.** Should medical marijuana be legalized?

Answers

8. B. The word *lousy* makes it hard to say you liked it; you'd be admitting to liking lousy films.

9. U.

10. B. Most people probably would not feel comfortable answering *yes* to this question.

11. B. A *yes* answer means you support the destruction of natural resources.

12. U.

Practice

To further improve your critical thinking and reasoning skills, take each of the unbiased questions from items 8 through 12 and turn them into biased questions. Then do the opposite: Take the biased questions and turn them into fair questions. Write your answers on a separate piece of paper.

Answers

Your answers will vary, but your revised questions should look something like this:

8. What did you think of that movie?

9. Don't you think that teenagers are too irresponsible to be allowed to drive until they're 18?

10. Are you going to vote to reelect the governor?

11. Do you support rainforest harvesting?

12. Do you think that medical marijuana, which dramatically relieves the pain and suffering of cancer and glaucoma patients, should be legalized?

In Short

Euphemisms, dysphemisms, and *biased questions* can have a powerful influence on victims, suspects, and juries. Euphemisms replace negative expressions with ones that are neutral or positive. Dysphemisms do the opposite: They replace neutral or positive expressions with ones that are harsh or negative. Biased questions make it difficult for us to answer questions fairly. Learning to recognize these subtle persuasion techniques promotes independent thinking and lets people come to their own conclusions, rather than the conclusions others want them to reach. In law enforcement, all testimony must be as free from bias as possible.

SKILL BUILDING UNTIL NEXT TIME

- Listen carefully to conversations, to the news, to what people say to you and ask of you. Do you notice any euphemisms, dysphemisms, or biased questions? Do you catch yourself using any of these techniques yourself?

- You can improve your ability to recognize subtle persuasion techniques by practicing them yourself. Come up with euphemisms, dysphemisms, and biased questions throughout the day.

Working with Arguments

LESSON SUMMARY

You hear arguments of all kinds throughout the day. In this lesson, you'll learn how to recognize the components of a deductive argument and how it differs from an inductive argument.

I n law enforcement, all conclusions must be supported by evidence. Action taken without supporting evidence or justification is likely to be viewed as improper and can even be characterized as a dereliction of duty. The old maxim, "Because I said so!" may have suited your parents well, but it will not serve you well in your law enforcement career. This is especially true when you are documenting your actions in official reports. It's important to provide qualifiable reasons for your actions and conclusions. By providing qualifiable reasons, you can best justify your actions and *support* your argument.

In the next three lessons, you're going to learn about **deductive arguments**: what they are, how they work, and how to recognize (and make) a good deductive argument—one that supports its assertions. First, you need to know what *deductive reasoning* is. To help define it, the counterpart of deductive reasoning, which is *inductive reasoning*, will be introduced first. Inductive reasoning is equally important because this is the reasoning pattern utilized most by law enforcement officers. Inductive reasoning is covered in more depth in a later lesson.

Inductive Reasoning

When detectives arrive at the scene of a crime, the first thing they do is look for clues that can help them piece together what happened. A broken window, for example, might suggest how a burglar entered or exited. Likewise, the fact that an intruder didn't disturb anything but a painting that hid a safe might suggest that the burglar knew exactly where the safe was hidden. And this, in turn, suggests that the burglar knew the victim. The process described here is called **inductive reasoning**. It consists of making observations and then drawing conclusions based on those observations. Like a detective, you use inductive reasoning all the time in your daily life. You might notice, for example, that every time you eat a hot dog with chili and onions, you get a stomachache. Using inductive reasoning, you could logically conclude that the chili dogs cause indigestion, and that you should probably stop eating them. Similarly, you might notice that your cat tries to scratch you every time you rub her stomach. You could logically conclude that she does not like her stomach rubbed. In both examples, what you're doing is moving from the *specific*—a particular observation—to the *general*—a larger conclusion. Inductive reasoning starts from observation and evidence and leads to a conclusion. Using inductive reasoning generally involves the following questions:

1. What have you observed? What evidence is available?
2. What can you conclude from that evidence?
3. Is that *conclusion* logical?

We'll come back to these questions in a later lesson. For now, you know enough about inductive reasoning to see how deductive reasoning differs from it.

Deductive Reasoning

Unlike inductive reasoning, which moves from *specific evidence* to a *general conclusion*, **deductive reasoning** does the opposite; it generally moves from a *conclusion* to the *evidence* for that conclusion. In inductive reasoning, the conclusion has to be "figured out" and we must determine whether the conclusion is valid. In deductive reasoning, on the other hand, we start with the conclusion and then see whether the *evidence* for that conclusion is valid. Generally, if the evidence is valid, the conclusion it supports is valid as well. In other words, deductive reasoning involves asking:

1. What is the conclusion?
2. What evidence supports it?
3. Is that *evidence* logical?

If you can answer yes to question 3, then the conclusion should be logical and the argument sound. It's easy to confuse inductive and deductive reasoning, so here's something to help you remember which is which:

Inductive: Evidence • Conclusion (IEC)
Deductive: Conclusion • Evidence (DCE)

Inductive reasoning starts with the evidence and moves to the conclusion. Deductive reasoning begins with the conclusion and moves to the evidence for that conclusion. Here's a memory trick to help you: You can remember that the word *Inductive* begins with a vowel, as does *Evidence*, so in inductive reasoning, you start with the evidence. *Deductive* begins with a consonant, and so does *Conclusion*, which is where you begin in deductive reasoning.

In the field of logic, deductive reasoning includes *formal* (mathematical or symbolic) logic such as syllogisms and truth tables. Some practice with formal logic will certainly sharpen your critical thinking and reasoning skills, but this book does not cover that kind of logic. Instead, continue to focus on *informal* logic—that is, the kind of critical thinking and reasoning skills that help you solve problems, assess and defend arguments, and make effective decisions in your daily life.

The Parts of a Deductive Argument

Lesson 2, "Problem-Solving Strategies," talked about the importance of identifying the main issue in order to solve a problem. You learned to ask yourself, "What is the real problem to be solved here?" Then you took that problem and broke it down into its parts.

In looking at deductive arguments, you should follow a similar process. First, you should identify the conclusion. The **conclusion** is the main claim or point the argument is trying to make. The various pieces of evidence that support that conclusion are called **premises**. Keep in mind that an argument is not necessarily a fight. In talking about inductive and deductive reasoning, an **argument** refers to a claim that is supported by evidence. Whether that evidence is good is another matter!

Identifying the conclusion is often more difficult than you might expect, because conclusions can sometimes seem like premises, and vice versa. Another difficulty is that you're used to thinking of conclusions as coming at the end of something. But in deductive arguments, the conclusion can appear anywhere. Thus, when someone presents you with a deductive argument, the first thing you should do is ask yourself: "What is the main claim, or overall idea, that the argument is trying to prove?" In other words, just as a problem is often composed of many parts, the conclusion in a deductive argument is often composed of many premises. So it's important to keep in mind the big picture.

> **Claim:** assertion about the truth, existence, or value of something
> **Argument:** a claim supported by evidence
> **Conclusion:** the main claim or point in an argument
> **Premises:** pieces of evidence that support the conclusion

The Structure of Deductive Arguments

The conclusion in a deductive argument can be supported by premises in two different ways. Say you have an argument with three premises supporting the conclusion. In one type of deductive argument, each premise provides its own individual support for the conclusion. That is, each premise alone is evidence for that main claim. In the other type of argument, the premises work together to support the conclusion. That is, they work like a chain of ideas to support the argument. These two types of arguments are represented as diagrams next.

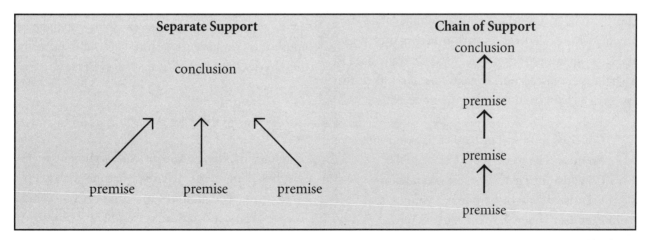

Here's how these two structures might look in a real argument.

Separate support: You shouldn't take that job. The pay is lousy, the hours are terrible, and there are no benefits.

You shouldn't take that job.

↑   ↑   ↑

Lousy   Terrible   No
pay   hours   benefits

Chain of support: You shouldn't take that job. The pay is lousy, which will make it hard for you to pay your bills, and that will make you unhappy.

You shouldn't take that job.

↑

and that will make you unhappy

↑

which will make it hard for you to pay your bills

↑

the pay is lousy

Notice how, in the second version, the entire argument builds on one idea, the lousy pay, whereas in the first, the argument is built on three separate ideas. Both, however, are equally logical.

Of course, an argument can have both separate and chain of support. You'll see an example of that shortly. What's important now is to understand that when premises depend on each other, as they do in the chain of support structure, what we really have is a chain of premises and conclusions. Look how the layers of a chain of support argument work:

Conclusion: It will be hard to pay your bills.
Premise: The pay is lousy.
Conclusion: That will make you unhappy.
Premise: It will be hard to pay your bills.
Premise: That will make you unhappy.

Overall conclusion: You shouldn't take that job. Because deductive arguments often work this way, it's very important to be able to distinguish the *overall* conclusion from the conclusions that may be used in the chain of support.

Identifying the Overall Conclusion

Read the following sentences:

He is a drug dealer, so he must be selling drugs. All known drug dealers sell drugs on this street.

These two sentences represent a small deductive argument. It's not a particularly *good* argument, but it is a good example of deductive structure. If these two sentences are broken down into their parts, three different claims arise:

1. He is a drug dealer.
2. He must be selling drugs.
3. All known drug dealers sell drugs on this street.

Now ask the key question: "What is this argument trying to prove?" In other words, what is the conclusion? Two clues should help you come up with the right answer. First, look at which claims have support (evidence) in this example. Is there anything here to support the claim that "He is a drug dealer"? No. Is there anything to support the claim, "All known drug dealers sell drugs on this street"? No. But there *are* premises to support the claim, "He must be selling drugs." Why must he be selling drugs? Because:

1. He is a drug dealer.
2. All known drug dealers sell drugs on this street.

Therefore, the conclusion of this argument is: "He must be selling drugs." That is what the writer is trying to prove. The premises that support this conclusion are "He is a drug dealer" and "All known drug dealers sell drugs on this street." A second clue in the conclusion that "He must be selling drugs" is the word *so*. Several key words and phrases indicate that a conclusion will follow. Similarly, certain words and phrases indicate that a premise will follow.

Indicate a Conclusion	Indicate a Premise
Accordingly	As indicated by
As a result	As shown by
Consequently	Because
Hence	For
It follows that	Given that
So	Inasmuch as
That's why	Since
Therefore	The reason is that
This shows/means/ suggests that	
Thus	

Now, are the premises that support the conclusion, "He must be selling drugs," separate support or chain of support? You should be able to see that these premises *work together* to support the conclusion. "He is a drug dealer" alone doesn't support the conclusion, and neither does "All known drug dealers sell drugs on this street." But the two premises together provide support for the conclusion. Thus, the example is considered a *chain of support* argument.

The Position of the Conclusion

While you might be used to thinking of the conclusion as something that comes at the end, in a deductive argument the conclusion can appear in different places. Here is the same argument rearranged in several different ways:

- He must be selling drugs. After all, he is a drug dealer, and all known drug dealers sell drugs on this street.
- All known drug dealers sell drugs on this street. Since he is a drug dealer, he must be selling drugs.

- He is a drug dealer, and all known drug dealers sell drugs on this street. He must be selling drugs.
- He must be selling drugs. After all, all known drug dealers sell drugs on this street, and he is a drug dealer.
- All known drug dealers sell drugs on this street. He must be selling drugs because he is a drug dealer.

In larger deductive arguments, especially the kind found in articles and essays, the conclusion will often be stated before any premises. This is also the case in a great deal of official reports and court paperwork prepared by law enforcement officers. But it's important to remember that the conclusion can appear anywhere in the argument. The key is to keep in mind what the argument *as a whole* is trying to prove. One way to test that you've found the right conclusion is to use the "because" test. If you've chosen the right claim, you should be able to put *because* between it and all the other premises. Thus:

He must be selling drugs **because** he is a drug dealer and **because** all known drug dealers sell drugs on this street.

Practice

Read the following short arguments carefully. First, separate the arguments into claims by putting a slash mark (/) between each claim. Then, identify the claim that represents the *conclusion* in each deductive argument by underlining that claim.

Example
We should go to the park. It's a beautiful day, and besides, I need some exercise.
We should go to the park. / It's a beautiful day / and besides, I need some exercise.

1. The roads are icy and it's starting to snow heavily. Stay in the guest bedroom tonight. You can leave early in the morning.

2. She's smart and she has integrity. She'd make a great councilwoman. You should vote for her.

3. I don't think you should drive. You'd better give me your keys. You had a lot to drink tonight.

4. You really should stop smoking. Smoking causes lung cancer and emphysema. It makes your clothes and breath smell like smoke. Besides, it's a waste of money.

Answers

Before you check your answers, use the "because" test to see if you've correctly identified the conclusion.

1. The roads are icy / and it's starting to snow heavily. / Stay in the guest bedroom tonight. / You can leave early in the morning.
2. She's smart / and she has integrity. / She'd make a great councilwoman. / You should vote for her.
3. I don't think you should drive. / You'd better give me your keys. / You had a lot to drink tonight.
4. You really should stop smoking. / Smoking causes lung cancer and emphysema. / It makes your clothes and breath smell like smoke. / Besides, it's a waste of money.

Practice

For each argument in items 1 through 4, identify whether the premises work as separate support or chain of support.

Answers

1. Separate. Three separate premises support the conclusion.
2. Separate and chain. "She's smart" and "she has integrity" are two separate claims that support the premise "She'd make a great council-woman." That premise, in turn, supports the conclusion.
3. Chain. The last premise, "You had a lot to drink tonight," supports the first, which in turn supports the conclusion.
4. Separate. Three separate premises support the conclusion.

In Short

Unlike inductive arguments, which move from evidence to conclusion, deductive arguments move from the conclusion to evidence for that conclusion. The **conclusion** is the overall claim or main point of the argument, and the claims that support the conclusion are called **premises**. Deductive arguments can be supported by premises that work alone (separate support) or together (chain of support). Law enforcement officers will make use of deduction from time to time. This will be done to support or overthrow a statement given by a suspect or witness. In your case, it will be very useful on your entrance exam.

SKILL BUILDING UNTIL NEXT TIME

- When you hear an argument, ask yourself whether it is an inductive or deductive argument. Did the person move from evidence to conclusion, or conclusion to evidence? If the argument is too complex to analyze this way, try choosing just one part of the argument and see whether it's inductive or deductive.
- When you come across deductive arguments today, try to separate the conclusion from the premises. Then consider whether the premises offer separate or chain of support.

Evaluating Evidence

LESSON SUMMARY

Since it's the *evidence* in a deductive argument that makes the conclusion valid, it's important to evaluate that evidence. This lesson shows you how to check premises for two key factors: credibility and reasonableness.

In Lesson 7, we discussed how to separate conclusions from the premises given in their support. It may not have been clear at the time, but this is a vital part of determining what actions we should take in our problem-solving and critical-thinking endeavors. This will also be invaluable to you in your future careers. As law enforcement officers, you will be called on to evaluate evidence every day. Before you accept any conclusion, therefore, you need to examine the *validity* of the evidence supporting that conclusion.

Specifically, there are three questions to ask yourself when evaluating evidence:

1. What type of evidence is offered?
2. Is that evidence *credible*?
3. Is that evidence *reasonable*?

Types of Evidence

Many different types of evidence can be offered in support of a conclusion. One of the most basic distinctions to make is between premises that are fact, premises that are opinion, and premises that can be accepted only as tentative truths.

Before going any further, here's a review of the difference between fact and opinion:

- A **fact** is something known for certain to have happened, to be true, or to exist.
- An **opinion** is something believed to have happened, to be true, or to exist.
- A **tentative truth** is a claim that may be a fact, but needs to be verified.

Whether they're facts, opinions, or tentative truths, premises can come in the following forms:

- statistics or figures
- physical evidence (artifacts)
- things seen, felt, or heard (observations)
- statements from experts and expert witnesses
- reports of experiences (eyewitnesses)
- ideas, feelings, or beliefs

Of course, some types of evidence seem more convincing than others. That is, people are often more likely to believe or be convinced by statistics than by someone's opinion. But that doesn't mean that all statistics should automatically be accepted and that all opinions should be rejected. Because statistics can be manipulated and because opinions can be quite reasonable, all forms of evidence need to be examined for both credibility and reasonableness.

For example, the *reasonableness* of statistics can't really be questioned, but their *credibility* must be questioned. Similarly, any feeling or belief should be examined for both credibility *and* reasonableness.

Is the Evidence Credible?

Whatever type of evidence is offered up, the first thing that needs to be considered is the credibility of the arguer/witness. Is the person making the argument/statement credible? Second, if the arguer/witness offers evidence from other sources, the credibility of those sources needs to be questioned. If both the arguer and his or her sources are credible, then the argument can tentatively be accepted. If not, the argument shouldn't be accepted until it is examined further.

First, here's a review of the criteria that determine credibility. To be credible, a source must:

- be free of bias
- have expertise

Expertise is determined by:

- education
- experience
- job or position
- reputation
- achievements

In the case of an eyewitness account, the following must be considered:

- the witness's potential for bias
- the environment
- the physical and mental condition of the witness
- the time between the event and recollection of the event

Here is a short deductive argument. Read the following passage carefully.

Current statistics show that 25% of relationships are affected by domestic violence. Approximately 2 million people a year fall victim to abuse by a spouse or significant other.

Domestic violence has been shown to have a significant effect on children who witness violent acts. In fact, children who witnessed intimate partner violence between their parents were 40% more likely to have behavioral problems in school. Witnessing domestic violence has also been shown to increase a child's reliance on physical violence and rage. In one study, it was demonstrated that four out of five male spousal abusers witnessed domestic violence as a child. If children exposed to domestic violence receive early counseling, many of these negative effects can be reversed and they can grow to have healthy adult relationships. That's why we must pass a law that requires mandatory family counseling for all families affected by domestic violence. We must take measures to improve the health and well-being of future generations to come. As a child, I witnessed an abusive relationship and have had to deal with the consequences of this.

Had early counseling been mandatory when I was a child, it might have saved me years of frustration and emotional unrest.

Note: The statistics in the foregoing passage and in the rest of the text are fictitious and meant to serve purely as examples.

First, identify the conclusion in this passage. What is the overall claim or point that the passage is trying to prove? Once you identify the conclusion, underline it.

You should have underlined the claim, "We must pass a law that requires mandatory family counseling for all families affected by domestic violence." The phrase "That's why" may have helped you identify this idea as the main claim. (If you had trouble, take a moment to review Lesson 7, "Working with Arguments.") The table lists the premises that support this conclusion. Note that not every sentence in this argument is a premise.

PREMISES THAT SUPPORT THE CONCLUSION	
TYPE OF PREMISE	PREMISE
Opinion	If children exposed to domestic violence receive early counseling, many of these negative effects can be reversed and they can grow to have healthy adult relationships.
Statistics	In fact, children who witnessed intimate partner violence between their parents were 40% more likely to have behavioral problems in school. Witnessing domestic violence has also been shown to increase a child's reliance on physical violence and rage. In one study, it was demonstrated that four out of five male spousal abusers witnessed domestic violence as a child.
Experience	As a child, I witnessed an abusive relationship and have had to deal with the consequences of this. Had early counseling been mandatory when I was a child, it might have saved me years of frustration and emotional unrest.

The arguer's experience offers an important clue here about *her* credibility. Because of what happened to her, is she likely to be biased on the issue? Absolutely. However, does this rule her out as a credible arguer? Not necessarily. Because of her experiences, chances are that she knows more about the issue than the average person. In other words, her experience indicates that she has some level of expertise in the area. Thus, though there's evidence of some bias, there's also evidence of some expertise. Because there is both bias and expertise, the argument needs to be examined further before you can determine whether to accept it.

Is the arguer's experience credible? Well, it can be assumed that she's telling the truth about her childhood. Is her opinion credible? That depends on her own credibility, which is still in question, and the reasonableness of that opinion, which is covered in the next section.

The next step is to consider the credibility of premises provided by the outside source; that is, the statistics offered about children who witness domestic violence. Notice that here the arguer doesn't give a source for the figures that she provides. This should automatically raise a red flag. Because numbers can so easily be manipulated and misleading, it's crucial to know the source of any figures offered in support of an argument.

Practice

1. Which of the following sources for the DUI statistic would you find most credible, and why?
   a. Mothers Against Drunk Driving
   b. National Highway Traffic Safety Administration
   c. The makers of Suds, the nation's best-selling beer

Answer

1. The most credible source is **b**, the National Highway Traffic Safety Administration. Of these three sources, this is by far the least biased. Mothers Against Drunk Driving has a position on alcohol availability and use, as do the makers of Suds, the nation's best-selling beer (most likely opposite the other two).

Is the Evidence Reasonable?

Now that you've considered the credibility of the arguer and the evidence she's offered, the next question you should ask is whether the evidence is *reasonable*. This question relates mostly to evidence in the form of opinions and tentative truths.

Remember that **reasonable** means *logical*: according to conclusions drawn from evidence or common sense. So whenever evidence comes in the form of an opinion or tentative truth, you need to consider how reasonable that premise is. Read this opinion:

> If children exposed to domestic violence receive early counseling, many of these negative effects can be reversed and they can grow to have healthy adult relationships.

Does this seem like a reasonable opinion to you? Why or why not?

However you feel about domestic violence, there *is* some sense to this opinion. After all, if children exposed to domestic violence received counseling, it seems logical that they would be able to deal better with their emotions and discern healthy reactions and relationships from unhealthy ones. Common sense, right?

But this opinion isn't a conclusion drawn from *evidence*. Look how much stronger this premise would be if it added *evidence* to *common sense*:

> If children exposed to domestic violence receive early counseling, many of these negative effects can be reversed and they can grow to have healthy adult relationships. For example, a program in New York City found that early counseling can reduce future violence by 73% as compared to those who did not receive counseling.

Notice that this statistic is used to support the opinion, which is then used to support the conclusion. In other words, this premise is part of a chain of support.

Opinions, then, can be reasonable either because they're based on common sense or because they're drawn from evidence. Of course, if an opinion is reasonable on *both* accounts, it's that much stronger as support for the conclusion.

Practice

Read the following opinions carefully. Are they reasonable? If so, is the reasonableness based on logic, common sense, or evidence?

2. You should not talk on a cell phone while driving. It is dangerous because it can distract drivers.

3. You should not talk on a cell phone while driving. The National Highway Traffic Safety Administration has demonstrated that drivers talking on cell phones have three times as many accidents than those who do not.

4. Don't listen to him. He's a jerk.

5. Don't listen to him. He gave me the same advice and it almost got me fired.

Answers

2. Reasonable, based on common sense.
3. Reasonable, based on evidence; in this case, on an expert's opinion.
4. Unreasonable. Because this is a deductive argument where the premise is unreasonable, the whole argument should be rejected as unreasonable.
5. Reasonable, based on evidence; in this case, on experience.

Practice

6. Reread the argument from the last lesson:

He is a criminal, so he must be selling drugs. All criminals sell drugs on this street.

Are the premises in this argument reasonable? Why or why not?

Answer

No, the premises in this argument are not reasonable, and therefore, the conclusion is not reasonable, either. Why not? Because common sense should tell you that you can't make big generalizations like "All criminals sell drugs." You should beware of any premise that makes a claim about *all* or *none*. There is almost always an exception.

In Short

The evaluation of evidence is a critical skill for law enforcement officers. Evidence can come in many forms, from statistics to feelings or opinions. When evaluating evidence, it's necessary to examine credibility and reasonableness: the credibility of the arguer, the credibility of any sources, and the reasonableness of each premise.

SKILL BUILDING UNTIL NEXT TIME

- As you hear deductive arguments throughout the day, pay attention to what type of evidence is offered in support of the conclusion. Statistics? Experiences? Opinions?
- Consider the credibility of the people who present you with deductive arguments today. Could they be biased? What is their level of expertise? If they offer other sources to support their arguments, are those sources credible?

Recognizing a Good Argument

LESSON SUMMARY

There are many components of a good argument—one that is convincing for good reason. This lesson shows you how to recognize and make a strong deductive argument.

Y ou are a jury member in the most contested criminal trial of the year. A prominent doctor stands accused of killing his wife. The prosecutor is giving his closing arguments. He says, "All the evidence points to one clear verdict and that is guilty! Dr. Smith clearly had motive and opportunity. Several expert witnesses gave testimony linking physical evidence found at the crime scene with Dr. Smith." Should you find in favor of the prosecution? Did the prosecutor make a good argument? How can you tell?

You already know what a deductive argument is. You know how to separate the conclusion from the evidence. And you know how to evaluate the evidence. These are essential steps in analyzing a deductive argument. But in order to determine the overall strength of an argument, there are several other criteria to take into consideration. Specifically, in a good deductive argument:

- The conclusion and premises are clear and complete.
- The conclusion and premises are free of excessive subtle persuasion.

- The premises are credible and reasonable.
- The premises are sufficient and substantive.
- The argument considers the other side.

You should already be familiar with the first three criteria, so we'll just take a moment to review them before we address the last two.

Clear and Complete

In Lesson 5, "Partial Claims and Half-Truths," you learned how to recognize hidden agendas. In order for a deductive argument to carry weight, its conclusion must be clear and complete; there should be no doubt about the claim being made. The same goes for the premises; if a comparison isn't fair or if what is being compared isn't clear, that claim cannot be valid. Evidence can't be reasonable if it is incomplete.

Free of Excessive Subtle Persuasion

In Lesson 6, "What's in a Word?" you learned about euphemisms, dysphemisms, and biased questions. These subtle persuasion techniques are indeed manipulative, but they're not the ultimate sin when it comes to arguments. It's natural for people to choose words that will have a certain impact on their listeners. It's natural, for example, for the government to use the phrase "military campaign" if they don't want to raise protests about going to war or for prisoners to have a "peaceful demonstration" rather than a riot. In other words, the *occasional* euphemism, dysphemism, or *mildly* biased question can be forgiven. But if an argument is loaded with these persuasive techniques, you should analyze it carefully. Generally, arguments that are laden with euphemisms, dysphemisms, and biased questions are this way because they lack reasonable and credible evidence. In other words, the arguer may be trying to persuade you with

language rather than reason because he or she lacks evidence. Excessive use of subtle persuasion can also indicate that the arguer is biased about the issue.

Credible and Reasonable Premises

As discussed in the previous lesson, the two criteria for good evidence are *credibility* and *reasonableness*. Evidence is credible when it is free of bias and when the sources have a respectable level of expertise. Evidence is reasonable when it is logical, drawn from evidence or common sense.

Sufficient and Substantive Premises

You are a corrections officer at a state prison. An inmate whom you know well and have a great working relationship with tells you to be careful in the mess hall. As you are walking him to the yard he tells you, "C.O., be careful when you're in the mess hall. Word is there's going to be a big fight soon."

Has he given you a good argument? Well, the conclusion, "be careful when you're in the mess hall," is clear and complete. The premise that supports the conclusion, "Word is there's going to be a big fight soon," is also clear and complete. The premise and conclusion are free from subtle persuasion. The premise is reasonable, and you don't have any reason to doubt credibility—he's given reliable information about prisons fights before. But is this a good argument? Yes, it is. As a law enforcement officer, you must place your personal safety above all other aspects of your work. The information provided by your informant should be taken seriously, but can it serve as the basis for official action? In some cases yes and in some no. For instance, if you are a police officer and a confidential informant tells you that someone on the corner of Prince Street and Main Street is selling drugs, would it justify you searching all people standing at that corner? Absolutely not!

Although all the other criteria check out, this statement has a very important weakness: It simply doesn't offer enough evidence. Not enough reasons are given to accept the conclusion. There may be 20 people standing on the corner. Not every one of them is selling drugs. In the case of the corrections officer, because of the level of danger inherent in the job, you may want to take the information provided seriously. This would still not justify you placing all prisoners in administrative lockdown for an extended period of time. If more information was provided in each example, it might make the conclusions much easier to accept. The following argument does a better job of supporting more aggressive enforcement action. What makes it better is the number of premises offered to support the conclusion. Some premises are separate support, and some are offered to support other premises (chains of support).

> C.O., watch out when you're in the mess hall. Word is there's going to be a big fight soon. The Bloods are going after the Crips. That crazy Blood Shorty is supposed to shank the first Crip he sees. Word is it's going to happen tonight."

Now *this* sounds like some information that should be acted on, doesn't it? What's good about this argument is not only that it offers several distinct premises that separately support the conclusion (**major premises**), but it also offers support (**minor premises**) for each of those premises. Each major premise is followed by a specific detail that supports *that* premise. Here's how this argument maps out:

Conclusion: Watch out when you are in the mess hall.

Major premise: Word is there is going to be a big fight soon.

Minor premise: The Bloods are going to go after the Crips.

Minor premise: That crazy Blood Shorty is supposed to shank the first Crip he sees.

Practice

1. Take the following argument and make it substantial. Provide more evidence by adding major and minor supporting premises:

> Officer, someone on the corner of Prince Street and Main Street is selling drugs. You should arrest him.

Stronger argument:

_____

_____

_____

_____

_____

Answer

Your answer will vary depending on what premises you chose to support this argument. At any rate, your argument should be significantly longer than the first version. Here's one revision that provides several major and minor premises to support the conclusion. The major premises are in bold.

> Officer, someone on the corner of Prince Street and Main Street is selling drugs. **Shorty is dealing drugs.** I saw him sell a twenty-bag to another guy. The guy handed him a $20 bill and he gave him a bag filled with powder. **You should arrest him.** He is messing up this community and getting our kids addicted. He is dangerous.

Considering the Other Side

At the beginning of the lesson, you were a jury member in the most contested criminal trial of the year. The prosecuting attorney was delivering his closing arguments and was attempting to sway you to believe his version of the argument. Did he provide a good argument based on the criteria we've discussed so far? Here's his argument again to refresh your memory:

> "All the evidence points to one clear verdict and that is guilty! Dr. Smith clearly had motive and opportunity. Several expert witnesses gave testimony linking physical evidence found at the crime scene with Dr. Smith."

Well, his argument is reasonable, credible, free of subtle persuasion, and he offers three different reasons, though they could be supported with specific details (minor premises). Still, this argument lacks one criterion of a good argument—it does not consider counterarguments.

Counterarguments are those arguments that might be offered by someone arguing for the other side. That is, if you are arguing that it's better to live in the city than in the country, you need to keep in mind what someone arguing that living in the country is better than living in the city might think. By considering counterarguments, you show your critical thinking skills—whatever your opinion, you have considered all sides of the issue. And this helps demonstrate your credibility, too; it shows that you've done your homework, that you obviously know something about the issue.

For example, when you hear the prosecuting attorney's argument, what thoughts might go through your mind? You might come up with the following reasons to vote guilty rather than not guilty:

- His DNA was found on the murder weapon.
- He was involved in an affair with his secretary.
- He was in financial debt and stands to get $1 million from his wife's life insurance.

Practice

A more detailed closing argument for the murder trial is printed next. Play devil's advocate and make a list of counterarguments that might be raised by the defense. Then rewrite the argument to make it stronger.

All the evidence points to one clear verdict and that is guilty! Dr. Smith clearly had motive and opportunity. He purchased the murder weapon, a meat cleaver, two days before the murder. Several expert witnesses gave testimony linking physical evidence found at the crime scene with Dr. Smith. His DNA and fingerprints were found on the murder weapon. The bloody shoeprint found in the garage was matched to a pair of shoes he owns and several witnesses testified that they had heard Dr. Smith talking about getting rid of his wife for months prior to her murder.

2. **Counterarguments:**

   _____

   _____

   _____

   _____

   _____

3. **Revised argument:**

   _____

   _____

   _____

   _____

   _____

Answer

Your counterarguments might look something like the following:

  a. He purchased the meat cleaver because he was preparing a special meal.
  b. His DNA was on the cleaver because he cut himself when he was cooking the meal.
  c. His fingerprints are on the cleaver because he used it to cook the meal.
  d. The witnesses misunderstood what Dr. Smith said, he was talking about getting rid of his wife's cat.

Your revised argument depends upon your counterarguments. Here's how the counterarguments might be incorporated. The sentences that address counterarguments are in bold.

All the evidence points to one clear verdict and that is guilty! Dr. Smith clearly had motive and opportunity. He purchased the murder weapon, a meat cleaver, two days before the murder. **Some may not find this so unusual, but Dr. Smith already owned a perfectly good meat cleaver.** Several expert witnesses gave testimony linking physical evidence found at the crime scene with Dr. Smith. His DNA and fingerprints were found on the murder weapon. **The knife was clean and showed no evidence of being used for cooking.** The bloody shoeprint found in the garage was matched to a pair of shoes he owns and several witnesses testified that they had heard Dr. Smith talking about getting rid of his wife for months prior to her murder. **They all testified to the fact that they distinctly heard him say, "I need to get rid of my wife. She needs to disappear."**

In Short

Strong deductive arguments meet the following criteria:

- The conclusion and premises are clear and complete.
- The conclusion and premises are free of excessive subtle persuasion.
- The premises are credible and reasonable.
- The premises are sufficient and substantive.
- The argument considers the other side.

The more of these criteria your arguments meet, the more convincing you'll be.

SKILL BUILDING UNTIL NEXT TIME

- Practice building your argument skills by playing devil's advocate. When you hear a deductive argument, think about what someone taking the opposite position might argue.
- When you hear or make an argument today, try to add more support to that argument. Add another major premise or add minor premises to support the major premises.

10 ▶ Putting It All Together

LESSON SUMMARY
This lesson puts together the strategies and skills you learned in Lessons 1 through 9. You'll review the key points of each lesson and practice evaluating claims and arguments.

Before going any further, it's time to review what you've learned in the preceding lessons so that you can combine strategies and put them to practical use. Repetition will help solidify ideas about what makes a good argument. Let's go through the lessons one at a time.

Lesson 1: Critical Thinking and Reasoning Skills

You learned that critical thinking means carefully considering a problem, claim, question, or situation in order to determine the best solution. You also learned that reasoning skills involve using good sense and basing reasons for doing things on facts, evidence, or logical conclusions. Finally, you learned that critical thinking and reasoning skills will help you compose strong arguments, assess the validity of other people's arguments, make more effective and logical decisions, and solve problems and puzzles more efficiently and effectively.

Lesson 2: Problem-Solving Strategies

You learned that the first step in solving any problem is to clearly identify the main issue and then break the problem down into its various parts. Next, you need to prioritize the issues and make sure that they're all relevant.

Lesson 3: Thinking versus Knowing

You practiced distinguishing between fact and opinion. Facts are things known for certain to have happened, to be true, or to exist. Opinions are things *believed* to have happened, to be true, or to exist. Tentative truths are claims that are thought to be facts, but need to be verified.

Lesson 4: Who Makes the Claim?

You learned how to evaluate the credibility of a claim by learning how to recognize bias and determine the level of expertise of a source. You also learned why eyewitnesses aren't always credible.

Lesson 5: Partial Claims and Half-Truths

You practiced identifying incomplete claims like those in advertisements. You also learned how averages can be misleading.

Lesson 6: What's in a Word?

You learned how euphemisms, dysphemisms, and biased questions can be used to get people to react in a certain way. Euphemisms replace negative expressions with positive ones; dysphemisms replace neutral or positive expressions with negative ones; and biased questions make it difficult for you to answer questions fairly.

Lesson 7: Working with Arguments

You learned that deductive arguments move from a conclusion to supporting evidence, or premises. You practiced identifying the conclusion and learned the difference between premises that provide separate support and those that are part of a chain of support.

Lesson 8: Evaluating Evidence

You practiced looking carefully at evidence to determine whether it is valid. The two key criteria you analyzed were credibility and reasonableness.

Lesson 9: Recognizing a Good Argument

Finally, you learned what makes a good argument: a conclusion and premises that are clear, complete, and free of excessive subtle persuasion; premises that are credible, reasonable, sufficient, and substantive; and a consideration of the other side.

If any of these terms or strategies sound unfamiliar to you, STOP. Take a few minutes to review whatever lessons remain unclear.

Practice

Let's utilize some of the skills that were discussed in the first nine lessons to answer typical reasoning questions found on various law enforcement entrance exams. These questions are examples of the types of critical thinking/logical reasoning questions that you will encounter on police, probations, corrections, and federal law enforcement entrance exams. Make every attempt to simulate a real-life testing environment. Find a quiet space and time yourself. Good luck.

Select the most appropriate answer that follows each question.

1. Agent Smith is in charge of all canine teams in his sector. Fifteen canine teams are stationed in his sector. Most of the canine teams are located at stations along the border. Several canine teams are located away from the border in large urban areas. All the teams must be available to travel to any duty station within the sector. *From the information given, it can be validly concluded that*, in Agent Smith's sector,
   a. most of the canine teams are located away from the border in large urban areas.
   b. only teams located along the border must be available to travel to any duty station within the sector.
   c. teams in urban areas do not need to be available to travel to other duty stations within the sector.
   d. none of the teams are exempt from traveling to any duty location within the sector.
   e. few of the canine teams are located at stations along the border.

2. The chief of police strives to provide quality service to the community while using resources efficiently. Accordingly, the chief must take into account several factors when allocating resources. For example, if it is a holiday weekend, additional staff are assigned to duty. However, if additional staff members are assigned to duty, special funding is needed from the city council. *From the information given, it can be validly concluded that,*
   a. if it is a holiday weekend, special funding is not needed from the city council.
   b. if it is not a holiday weekend, special funding is needed from the city council.
   c. if special funding is not needed from the city council, it is not a holiday weekend.
   d. if special funding is needed from the city council, it is a holiday weekend.
   e. if special funding is not needed from the city council, it is a holiday weekend.

3. Several different means of smuggling, such as cross-border tunnels, are used to bring narcotics, individuals, and contraband into the United States. Cross-border tunnels can be found all along the land border of the United States. They vary significantly in size and complexity of construction, although most are crudely constructed. Further, most cross-border tunnels are used for smuggling narcotics, although illegal aliens and other contraband have also been smuggled using tunnels. *From the information given, it CANNOT be validly concluded that*
   a. most cross-border tunnels are not skillfully constructed.
   b. all cross-border tunnels are used for narcotics smuggling.
   c. at least some cross-border tunnels are not free from narcotics smuggling.
   d. at least some of the means used for narcotics smuggling are cross-border tunnels.
   e. at least some means used for narcotics smuggling involve crudely constructed tunnels.

4. Although the owner of a certain farm said that all her Central American (for example, Salvadoran and Honduran) workers were working legally, border patrol agents discovered that many of the farm's employees were not authorized to work in the United States. After checking the employees' documentation, border patrol agents discovered that all the female employees were working in the United States legally and none of the illegal workers were from Honduras. *From the information given, it can be validly concluded that,* concerning the employees on this farm,
   a. all the employees from Honduras were working legally.
   b. some of the women were illegal workers.
   c. none of the employees from Honduras were female.
   d. some of the female employees were from Honduras.
   e. all the Salvadoran employees were women.

5. The two ways of acquiring U.S. citizenship at birth are by place of birth and inheritance from U.S. citizen parents. Any child born in the United States while under American jurisdiction is a U.S. citizen at birth. Because foreign ambassadors are not subject to American jurisdiction, children born in the United States to foreign ambassadors do not obtain U.S. citizenship at birth. Children born overseas to U.S. citizen parents derive U.S. citizenship at birth, as long as the parents previously lived in the United States for a sufficient period of time. All others must naturalize to become citizens. J.B. was not a U.S. citizen at birth.

From the information given, it can be validly concluded that
   a. J.B. was born in the United States.
   b. J.B. was born overseas to U.S. citizen parents.
   c. J.B. was not born in the United States to U.S. citizen parents.
   d. J.B. was not born overseas to U.S. citizen parents.
   e. J.B. was born to U.S. citizen parents.

6. When officers must physically force entry into a home, they are required to ensure that the home is in a secure condition when they leave. Failure to secure the home leaves the officers liable for loss of items from the home and/or damage to the home that results from leaving the property unsecured. It is legal to break down doors in order to gain entry, if that degree of force is determined by an officer to be necessary. If an officer forces entry, the officer is required to take measures to minimize damage to the property. Officer Stoler needs to gain entry into a suspect's home. *From the information given, it CANNOT be validly concluded that*
   a. Officer Stoler is required to minimize damage to the home if Officer Stoler forces entry.
   b. if Officer Stoler is not required to ensure that the home is secure upon leaving, then Officer Stoler did not force entry into the home.
   c. if Officer Stoler forces entry and fails to secure the home, Officer Stoler may be liable for loss of items resulting from leaving the home unsecured.
   d. if Officer Stoler must physically force entry into the home, then Officer Stoler is not required to ensure that the home is secure upon leaving.
   e. Officer Stoler will be required to secure the home unless Officer Stoler does not force entry.

7. Recently, border patrol agents received leads from informants about possible illegal activity at La Rosita Park. When agents arrived at the park, they drove through the parking lots, looking for individuals and vehicles matching their leads. They examined several suspicious vehicles, including many unregistered vehicles. All the unregistered vehicles contained bundles of marijuana. No arrests have been made in connection with this incident. *From the information given, it can be validly concluded that*

a. several arrests have been made in connection with this incident.

b. some of the vehicles that did not contain bundles of marijuana were unregistered.

c. all the vehicles that contained bundles of marijuana were unregistered.

d. all the vehicles that did not contain bundles of marijuana were registered.

e. some of the vehicles that contained bundles of marijuana were registered.

8. When an illegal alien is being removed, the alien's passport in U.S. government possession is returned to the issuing government, not to the illegal alien. If the illegal alien's departure is voluntary, the passport is allowed to be returned to the alien. The U.S. government holds the passport of H.B., an illegal alien who must leave the country. *From the information given, it CANNOT be validly concluded that*

a. H.B.'s departure is not voluntary if H.B.'s passport is allowed to be returned to H.B.

b. if H.B.'s passport is not returned to the issuing government upon H.B.'s departure, then H.B. is not being removed.

c. H.B.'s departure is not voluntary unless the passport is allowed to be returned to H.B.

d. if H.B.'s passport is not allowed to be returned to H.B., then H.B.'s departure is not voluntary.

e. if H.B. is being removed, then H.B.'s passport is to be returned to the issuing government.

9. Oleoresin capsicum (OC), or pepper spray, is an effective law enforcement tool for incapacitating violent or threatening arrestees without using deadly force. Pepper spray causes a burning sensation of the eyes and skin and tearing and swelling of the eyes. Almost all arrestees are unable to see after being sprayed with OC. Some law enforcement agencies that have adopted OC sprays have fewer allegations of use of excessive force. Many law enforcement agencies have reported a reduction in officer and arrestee injuries as a result of the introduction of OC sprays. *From the information given, it can be validly concluded that*

a. any use of a law enforcement tool that causes a burning sensation of the eyes is considered to be the use of deadly force.

b. few arrestees are able to see after being sprayed with OC.

c. all law enforcement agencies that have reduced officer and arrestee injuries have also reduced allegations of use of excessive force.

d. no agencies that have adopted OC sprays have fewer allegations of use of excessive force.

e. only pepper spray is an effective law enforcement tool for incapacitating violent or threatening arrestees without using deadly force.

10. "The hole" is a common term officers use to describe a holding cell where inmates with behavioral problems are placed for disciplinary isolation. Which situation would cause Officer Campbell to consider placing an inmate in the hole?

   a. Inmate Garvey is tired of standing in line for his haircut. He walks to the front of the line and punches inmate Douglas in the nose before pushing him out of his way.

   b. Inmate Witte is arguing with inmate Alvarez. She tells inmate Alvarez that she is stupid and then turns and walks away.

   c. A food fight breaks out in the cafeteria, but Officer Campbell cannot ascertain who started it.

   d. A new regulation limiting inmate access to weights in the gym has come out, and inmate Jackson is angry about it. He says he will be filing a grievance with the warden's office.

11. Vehicles entering and leaving prison facilities should be checked thoroughly. Officers on duty at the gates should check the identities of all occupants of the vehicles, and vehicles exiting the area should be checked for possible escapees. Officer Shakley is standing guard at Gate 1. Which situation would cause her to check the vehicle and its occupants particularly carefully?

   a. A solitary man in a two-door convertible drives up to the gate. He presents identification that shows he is an attorney and says he has come to meet with an inmate.

   b. A large delivery van is in the line of cars waiting to exit the facility. The driver, who entered the facility laughing and joking, looks tense and rigid as he approaches the gate.

   c. A corrections officer in uniform approaches the gate on a touring motorcycle.

   d. A prison employee driving a station wagon approaches the gate to exit the facility.

12. Random bed checks during the night are conducted by officers to make sure inmates are where they are supposed to be and to check on the condition and behavior of inmates. Officer Quinton is conducting a bed check and is carefully checking for "living breathing flesh." Which situation would cause him to check more closely?

   a. When checking one of the cells, he sees a lump under the blanket in the middle of one bunk but does not see a head on the pillow.

   b. In another cell, he sees the inmate lying on his stomach with his face turned away and with one foot hanging off the side of his bed.

   c. In yet another cell, he sees the inmate lying on his back on top of the blanket on his bunk with one arm flung across his face.

   d. In a fourth cell, he sees the inmate lying on the cement floor with his shirt off, snoring loudly.

13. Searches for possible weapons and contraband are essential for the safety and security of the facility. Inmates know that these searches, often called shakedowns, of their cells and dormitories are part of prison routine. If an officer expects to get the maximum result from a shakedown, the officer should do which of the following?

a. make an announcement at breakfast that shakedowns will occur all that day and ask for inmates to come forward voluntarily with any contraband or weapons

b. schedule a time with each inmate to go through his possessions

c. conduct searches each night one hour before the inmates are locked down for the night

d. conduct searches randomly, at different times, and on different days

14. Report writing is a critical element of a corrections officer's job. Officers are expected to write detailed reports that tell who, what, when, where, how, and why. Reports are to be written whenever an incident occurs that should be documented, a violation of the rules and/or law occurs, or an official action is taken by a corrections officer. Which situation would most likely cause an officer to write a report?

a. Every Tuesday the library remains open an extra hour for those inmates who want to conduct research for their court cases. Today it closes early, and several inmates complain loudly as they gather up their materials to leave.

b. Inmate Rossie punches inmate Browder during an argument and starts a fight that lasts a couple of minutes. Inmate Browder tells the investigation officer that it wasn't important and he doesn't want the incident to be investigated.

c. Inmates in the day room are having a heated discussion about who is going to win the World Series this year. Inmate Sebghati pounds the table and shouts.

d. Inmates waiting to use the outdoor recreational yard are told to wait until the rain stops. They grumble among themselves, and inmate Forbes yells to a corrections officer that she wants to go out in the rain.

15. Some corrections officers are required to deal with the public as well as with the inmate population during the course of their work. Officers are expected to treat visitors courteously and respectfully but are required to take action if visitors to the facility behave in a suspicious manner or fail to abide by the rules and regulations. Which situation should cause an officer to become suspicious of a visitor?

a. A visitor to the facility tries to make a wrong turn when he passes through the first gate. He tells the guard he failed to follow the signs because he can't read.

b. A visitor arrives too late for visitation hours and is angry when officers politely turn him away. He vows to write the warden to complain about his treatment.

c. Inmate Godwin's wife comes for a visit, becomes upset, and asks to leave the facility before her visitation time is up.

d. Cousin Jeremy arrives to see inmate Everson and is seen repeatedly shaking the inmate's hand in the visitor center.

16. It is important for corrections officers to develop a feel for the moods and behaviors of the inmates in their care. Whenever possible, officers should attempt to head off problems rather than wait for them to happen. Officer Riley notices that inmate Napier is edgy and has been arguing with anyone who tries to speak to him. What should Officer Riley do?

a. Take inmate Napier aside and try to find out what is bothering him.

b. Lock down the cellblock until inmate Napier is in a better mood.

c. Take inmate Napier to solitary confinement before any fighting breaks out.

d. Tell the other inmates to stay away from inmate Napier until his behavior improves.

17. Officers are expected to make frequent counts of inmates for the safety and security of the facility. During these counts, inmates are expected to follow the instructions of the officers who are conducting the count. An officer needs to conduct an inmate count at the recreation yard while a basketball game is in progress. How should she handle this situation?

a. She should let the game continue and count the players on the sidelines first and then the other players as they run past.

b. She should wait until the recreation time is over and count inmates as they come in from the yard.

c. She should stop the game, count all the inmates, and then let them resume the game.

d. She should ask each team to count their own players while she is watching.

18. Inmates have been known to befriend officers and then try to convince the officers to perform favors for them. After favors are performed, inmates often try to blackmail officers, knowing that the officers can face disciplinary action if their superiors find out that they performed the favors. Which situation should Officer Mendoza avoid?

a. Inmate Keiser asks Officer Mendoza to write out a pass for him to get a haircut. Officer Mendoza notices that the inmate's hair is well below his collar.

b. Inmate Mohammed asks Officer Mendoza for permission to go to the library to research court documents.

c. Inmate Saunders asks Officer Mendoza for more socks, because he is wearing his last pair.

d. Inmate Crowley asks Officer Mendoza to call his house once a day to check on his wife for him.

19. Lieutenant Magnus is attempting to determine which motorcycle officer to commend for issuing the most citations during the month. She knows that Officer Slack issued more citations than Officer Diamond, who issued 270. Officer Diamond issued 30 more than Officer Sharp, but ten fewer than officer than Officer Elia. How many citations did Officer Elia issue?

a. 270

b. 240

c. 280

d. 220

20. Officer DeMarco is on routine patrol at about 3 A.M. on a Sunday morning. He drives his police vehicle to the rear alley of a shopping center and discovers a man lying face down on the ground. Officer DeMarco approaches the man and finds that he is breathing. Officer DeMarco also sees drug paraphernalia, including a hypodermic syringe, on the ground next to the man. Officer DeMarco tries to wake the man, but is unable. What is Officer DeMarco's best course of action?

  a. presume the man is sleeping, move him out of the way of the alley traffic, and continue routine patrol
  b. arrest the man for possession of the drug paraphernalia
  c. call for an ambulance and have the man transported to a medical facility
  d. call for a supervisor

21. Four eyewitnesses saw a vehicle being stolen and noted the license plate number. Each wrote down a different number listed below. Which one is probably right?

  a. KLV 017
  b. XIW 007
  c. XIW 017
  d. XIV 017

22. Randy Wade comes home and surprises a burglar in his house. The burglar runs past Randy out the door. Which one of the following parts of Randy's description of the burglar will be most helpful to police in identifying him?

  a. He walked with a limp.
  b. He carried a VCR.
  c. He wore a ski mask.
  d. He smelled like fish.

23. Officer Madeira has noticed that daytime residential burglaries in her district have increased during the past two months. Which of the following situations, occurring around 1:00 P.M., should Officer Madeira investigate?

  a. a teenaged boy dancing down the sidewalk, holding a large radio to his ear and singing
  b. a woman walking door-to-door carrying a small suitcase
  c. a man parked in the shade eating a sandwich and watching some children play
  d. a man walking down the street carrying a medium-sized television set

Use the following information to answer questions 24 through 26.

Officers responding alone to the scene of a burglar alarm should do the following in the order given:

  1. Turn off siren and emergency lights as soon as possible to keep from alerting suspects.
  2. Park the patrol car away from the building.
  3. Notify the dispatcher of their arrival and location.
  4. Begin checking the outside of the building for signs of entry.
  5. Notify the dispatcher if signs of entry are discovered.
  6. Wait for backup if it is available before going inside a building where entry has been made.
  7. Tell backup officers where to position themselves as they arrive.

24. Officer Celer is on patrol by herself at about 4 A.M. She is driving down a residential street when she sees dark smoke coming out of a house. As she pulls to the curb, she observes a man carrying a gas can exit the house and run down the street. What is her best course of action?

a. Call for backup before pursuing the man with a gas can.

b. Notify dispatch of the fire, request backup, and pursue the man with the gas can.

c. Notify dispatch of the fire and the man running from the scene, then use the garden hose at the front of the house to fight the fire.

d. Notify dispatch about both the fire and the man running from the scene, then attempt to wake anyone in the house and render aid if it is safe to do so.

25. On a Sunday afternoon at about 2 P.M., Officer Dodrill is on routine patrol when he receives a radio call to respond to a silent burglary alarm in a commercial district. Dodrill knows that most of the businesses in that area are manufacturing firms that are generally closed on Sunday. Dodrill also knows that most silent burglary alarms are false activations. Which of the following is his best course of action?

a. Because most of the calls are false, he should ignore it and request a dinner break from dispatch.

b. Although most of the calls are false, the area is filled with closed manufacturing businesses, so he should activate his emergency lights and siren and proceed rapidly to the location.

c. Although most of the calls are false, he should proceed directly to the location.

d. Because most of the calls are false, he should continue to patrol his assigned area until he is nearer the location.

26. Officer Carmine was requested to transport two prisoners from the department holding facility to the county regional jail. After completing the transport, she checks the back seat of the police vehicle and notices two $10 bills. What is her best course of action?

a. Give the money to the regional jail personnel and tell them to give each prisoner $10.

b. Complete the appropriate department form explaining the circumstances and deposit the money with the department property or evidence officer.

c. Take the money and send it to a local charity.

d. Interview the prisoners and give the money to the one most likely to have misplaced it.

27. Downtown merchants have complained to Sergeant Ramos about a recent rash of auto thefts. Mr. Smith says that six of his best customers have had their cars stolen in the past two weeks while parked in the downtown area. Sergeant Ramos alerts Officer Hammond to patrol the area closely. Which following situation should Officer Hammond investigate?

a. a transient approaching people as they get out of their cars to ask them for a cigarette

b. two young men sitting on the hood of a car parked in front of Mr. Smith's store

c. a tow truck operator attempting to open the door of a vehicle for a man who is standing nearby

d. a man walking from parked car to parked car pulling on the door handles

28. Sergeant Janikowski is responsible for determining the vacation schedule for the coming year. According to the department vacation policy, choice of vacation is ranked according to seniority. Janikowski knows that Ducale is the least senior, James is more senior than Smyth, and Barton has less seniority than Smyth. Which officer should have first choice for his or her vacation?
   a. Ducale
   b. Smyth
   c. James
   d. Barton

29. Four people witnessed a mugging. Each gave a different description of the mugger. Which description is probably right?
   a. He was average height, thin, and middle-aged.
   b. He was tall, thin, and middle-aged.
   c. He was tall, thin, and young.
   d. He was tall, of average weight, and middle-aged.

30. Among other requirements, an applicant for citizenship must show that he or she is "attached to the principles of the Constitution of the United States and well-disposed to the good order and happiness of the United States." The courts have defined *attachment to the Constitution* as a belief in representative democracy, a commitment to the ideals embodied in the Bill of Rights, a belief that political change should be effected only in an orderly way, and general satisfaction with life in the United States. These requirements do *not*, however, preclude a belief that it might be desirable to make a change in our form of government as long as the change is made within constitutional limits. *From the information given, it can be validly concluded that*
   a. all persons who want the U.S. government to change should be denied citizenship.
   b. only persons who believe that it might be desirable to work toward change in the U.S. government should be granted citizenship.
   c. all persons who work within constitutional limits toward change in the U.S. government should be granted citizenship.
   d. a commitment to the ideals embodied in the Bill of Rights is only one aspect of *attachment to the Constitution.*
   e. *attachment to the Constitution* cannot include a belief that it might be desirable to change the form of government of the United States.

31. The United States is a country of immigrants who came to inherit the land neither by divine right nor by open immigration policy. Because the land was taken from indigenous inhabitants, it is wrong for current citizens to exclude future immigrants. However, some people believe that too much immigration may compromise the standard of living in the United States. As a result, jobs and resources may be taken from persons who are already citizens, so that the very reasons immigrants were historically attracted to the United States—that is, all its advantages and opportunities—may be threatened if the country becomes overcrowded. *From the information given, it can be validly concluded that*

a. because current citizens did not inherit this land by divine right, too much immigration may compromise the United States' standard of living.

b. if too much immigration would compromise the United States' standard of living, then its citizens should want an open immigration policy.

c. if the citizens of the United States want an open immigration policy, then the United States standard of living would not be compromised.

d. if the United States does not have an open immigration policy, then the land was taken away from its indigenous inhabitants.

e. some people believe the very reasons immigrants were historically attracted to the United States will be compromised by an open immigration policy.

32. The U.S. immigration laws are designed to protect the health, welfare, and security of the United States. Therefore, these laws prohibit the issuance of visas to applicants who fit within certain categories. Among those who must be refused visas are those with a communicable disease, those with a dangerous physical or mental disorder, those who have committed serious criminal acts, and those who have used illegal means to enter the United States. *From the information given, it can be validly concluded that*, under U.S. immigration laws,

a. everyone who is refused a visa has committed a serious criminal act.

b. no one who is refused a visa has a communicable disease.

c. everyone with a dangerous physical or mental disorder must be refused a visa.

d. using illegal means to enter the United States does not always prohibit issuance of a visa.

e. only those who meet these criteria will be denied visas.

33. If a state has the final authority to determine citizenship, this can result in some persons having dual nationalities and others being stateless. A child can be born stateless when two situations arise simultaneously—the state in which the child is born only recognizes the child as receiving the nationality of the parents, and the parents' home state only recognizes the nationality of the state where the child is born. *From the information given, it can be validly concluded that*, in the case of a child born in a state other than his parents' home state,

a. the child has dual nationality if the parent's home state recognizes only the nationality of the state where a child is born.

b. the child is considered to have dual nationality if the state in which he is born only recognizes a child as receiving the nationality of the parents.

c. the child is considered stateless if the state in which he is born and the parents' home state each only recognizes a child as receiving the nationality of the parents.

d. the child is considered stateless if his parents' home state only recognizes the child as receiving the nationality of the parents.

e. the child is considered to have dual nationality if the state where he was born recognizes the birthplace of the child and his parents' home state recognizes the nationality of the parents.

34. According to the Fourteenth Amendment to the U.S. Constitution, "No state shall make or enforce any law which shall abridge the privileges or immunities of citizens of the United States, nor shall any state deprive any person of life, liberty, or property, without due process of law; nor deny to any person within its jurisdiction the equal protection of the laws." *From the information given, it can be validly concluded that*

a. no state can abridge the privileges of its citizens under any circumstances.

b. states can abridge the privileges of its citizens without due process.

c. a state can abridge the privileges of its citizens only with due process.

d. the Constitution does not allow citizens and noncitizens to be treated differently.

e. equal protection of the laws is a privilege given to citizens only.

35. Criminals should be held accountable for their behavior. If holding criminals accountable for their behavior requires harsh sentencing, then so be it. However, no person should be held accountable for behavior over which he or she had no control. *From the information given, it can be validly concluded that*

a. criminals should not be held accountable for the behavior of other people.

b. people have control of their own behavior.

c. people cannot control the behavior of other people.

d. behavior that cannot be controlled should not be punished.

e. criminals have control over their own behavior that may subject them to harsh punishment.

36. Under Immigration and Nationality Act (INA) law, any alien who is believed likely to become a public charge is excludable at the time of application. However, in *Matter of Kohama* (1978), it was decided that an immigrating couple who had no means of support other than reliance on their daughter and son-in-law, who were U.S. residents, could not be excluded as likely to become public charges. The daughter and son-in-law gave depositions and submitted affidavits as evidence of their ability and willingness to support the couple. The court held that such evidence was sufficient to overcome the belief that they would become charges of the state. *From the information given, it can be validly concluded that*

   a. persons may be permitted to immigrate to the United States if they have relatives in their home country willing to support them.
   b. for the court to accept a claim that relatives will support an immigrant to the United States, the relatives must submit evidence supporting their ability to do so.
   c. if relatives agree to support a person and can submit evidence supporting their ability to do so, then that person must immigrate to the United States.
   d. if a person wishes to immigrate to the United States and has no relative willing and able to financially support him or her, then that person may not immigrate to the United States.
   e. if a person immigrates to the United States, he or she has relatives willing and able to support him or her.

37. One strategy for controlling the nation's borders involves demonstrating the futility of crossing the borders illegally. This sometimes requires border patrol agents to perform activities within the United States, away from the borders. Among the reasons they do this are to seek out and arrest aliens living illegally inside the United States, and to find and stop the modes of transportation used to transport illegal aliens across and within U.S. borders. *From the information given, it can be validly concluded that*

   a. controlling the nation's borders can occur only at the borders themselves.
   b. controlling the nation's borders can never occur at the borders themselves.
   c. border patrol agents' activities at the borders are more important than those away from the borders.
   d. border patrol agents' activities away from the borders are more important than those at the borders.
   e. activities at the borders and away from the borders work together to protect the nation's borders.

38. One concern of law enforcement officials is the risk of terrorists taking advantage of illegal immigration along the southern border and becoming lost in the flow of aliens entering the United States there. Focusing on the entrance of illegal aliens across U.S. borders might have the additional effect of impacting national security in a positive way. *From the information given, it can be validly concluded that*

   a. all terrorists are illegal aliens.
   b. all illegal aliens are terrorists.
   c. efforts to limit illegal immigration are likely to help deter terrorism.
   d. terrorists are entering the United States through the southern border.
   e. illegal aliens and terrorists work together to enter the United States illegally.

39. Protecting the United States' northern border presents unique challenges due to its length, geography, and weather. The solutions for protecting the northern border include a combination of maintaining sufficient workforce levels, improved communications and other technology, additional air assets, partnerships with state and local authorities, and use of checkpoints and other deterrents.

From the information given, it can be validly concluded that

   a. the challenges involved in protecting the northern border are mostly about maintaining workforce levels.

   b. any one solution to protect the northern border will go a long way toward achieving success.

   c. checkpoints and other deterrents have not been successful in the past.

   d. a combination of solutions to protect the northern border will likely be more successful than any one solution.

   e. relationships with Canadian officials are not an important factor in protecting the United States' northern border.

40. The legal authority of a border patrol agent is derived from congressional legislation; this is called *statutory authority*. However, Congress does not have the final word regarding the interpretation and application of legislation, as this power is reserved for the judicial branch of government. Following the codification of statutory authority, written guidance regarding the codified statutory authority is created by federal agencies and published and updated annually in the Federal Register; this is known as the Code of Federal Regulations. However, border patrol agents are ultimately required to operate in accordance with agency regulations or directives that are more restrictive than a plain reading of statutory law. Agency regulations and directives are promulgated by an agency to provide field-level guidance to agents to use when exercising their statutory authority. These regulations comply with the requirements of both statutory legislation and the Code of Federal Regulations. Additionally, the American judicial system is constantly rendering decisions that affect the interpretation and application of legislation enacted by Congress. Border patrol agents routinely receive legal updates regarding judicial decisions that ultimately decide how agents exercise their statutory authority in the field.

From the information given, it can be validly concluded that

   a. the legal authority of a border patrol agent is derived from agency directives.

   b. the legal authority of an agency to publish written guidance in the Federal Register is derived from statutory authority.

   c. the courts interpret and apply the Code of Federal Regulations in legal matters.

   d. statutory authority is interpreted through field-level agency regulations and directives.

   e. the judicial system ultimately interprets and applies congressional legislation, and these decisions affect the method and means by which border patrol agents exercise their statutory authority.

41. Technology can be of great value in protecting U.S. borders. Border patrol agents need to know how this technology works and when to use it. Among the tools available are remote video surveillance and sensing (RVSS) cameras, radiation detection equipment, satellite communications, and remote access to national law enforcement databases. These devices can give agents an advantage in keeping illegal immigrants out, and in apprehending them once they've entered the United States illegally. *From the information given, it can be validly concluded that*

a. technology is always an advantage in protecting U.S. borders.
b. protecting U.S. borders would be impossible without technology.
c. border patrol agents need to know how to use radiation detection equipment to be successful at their jobs.
d. technology is only as good as the agents who use it.
e. knowing what technology to use and how to use it is a valuable resource for agents, both in preventing illegal immigration and in apprehending illegal aliens.

42. Maintaining and knowing how to use firearms is important for all law enforcement officials. Many law enforcement officers say that they have never had to fire a weapon, even after many years on the job. Others report that they've found themselves in situations requiring that they use their weapon after only days or weeks on the job. Decisions an officer makes in a split second under life-and-death pressure may be analyzed and evaluated over the course of years. Extensive training in the use of firearms is critical to an officer making the best possible decision when called upon to do so. *From the information given, it can be validly concluded that*

a. firearms should never be used unless a superior orders an officer to do so.
b. firearms should never be used unless an officer's life is in immediate danger.
c. there is no way to know in advance if or how often a law enforcement officer will need to fire a weapon.
d. decisions made under pressure in a fraction of a second are never good decisions.
e. the best training always results in the best decision when it comes to using firearms.

43. Under INA law, unless an applicant for citizenship is physically unable to do so because of blindness or deafness, he or she must be able to speak, understand, read, and write simple English. Before 1978, the act provided an exemption to the literacy requirement for people who, on the effective date in 1952, were over 50 years of age and had been residing in the United States for periods totaling at least 20 years. In 1978, Congress amended the provision to exempt any person who was over the age of 50 at the time of filing a petition and who had been lawfully admitted for permanent residence for periods totaling 20 years. *From the information given, it can be validly concluded that*, on the effective date in 1952, all people over 50 years of age

a. became exempt from the literacy requirement unless they had lived in the United States for 20 years.
b. could become exempt from the literacy requirement if they had lived in the United States for 20 years.
c. had to meet the literacy requirements if they had lived in the United States for 20 years.
d. met the literacy requirements if they had lived in the United States for 20 years.
e. who had been in the United States at least 20 years met the literacy requirements.

44. Police Sergeant O'Malley reports that all police precincts in the city of Garrison have drug-seeking dogs, and that some police precincts in the same city have search-and-rescue dogs. Sergeant O'Malley professes to know all about dogs. Search-and-rescue dogs, he says, are better at tracking, but are disobedient, whereas drug-seeking dogs are obedient. All the precincts, Sergeant O'Malley maintains, have discontinued the use of attack dogs, because they are too dangerous. *From the information given, it CANNOT be validly concluded that,* according to Sergeant O'Malley,
   a. all police precincts have disobedient dogs.
   b. some police precincts have disobedient dogs.
   c. all police precincts have obedient dogs.
   d. no police precincts have attack dogs.
   e. no police precincts have dangerous dogs.

45. Under immigration law, one way a child under age 16 can receive a visa and be adopted is if that child is an orphan. A child is considered an orphan if both parents have died, disappeared, or abandoned the child, or if the sole or surviving parent is incapable of providing the child with proper care, and if that parent has irrevocably released the child for emigration and adoption. The orphan must be adopted by, or be traveling to the United States to be adopted by, a U.S. citizen and spouse jointly, or by an unmarried U.S. citizen at least 25 years of age. *From the information given, it can be validly concluded that* a child would be considered an orphan only if
   a. her parents are unable to care for her but will not release her for emigration and adoption.
   b. her parents are dead, or alive but have disappeared or abandoned her, or are unable to care for her and have released the child for emigration and adoption.

   c. she is adopted by spouses jointly.
   d. she is adopted by an unmarried single person over 25.
   e. she is under age 16 and her parents are dead.

46. Merchants in the South Oaks Shopping Mall are upset by a recent rash of purse snatchings in their parking lot. Officer Crandall is closely patrolling the mall area, including the vacant lot behind the stores. Which situation below would Officer Crandall most likely investigate?
   a. a car horn honking continuously in the mall parking lot
   b. a car in the mall parking lot with four flat tires and a broken windshield
   c. a woman's voice raised in anger in the mall parking lot
   d. a man running through the vacant lot with a bulky object under his sweatshirt

47. Drug addicts often try to pass fake prescriptions at pharmacies in order to get drugs illegally. Which of the following situations would lead an officer to investigate a possible forgery at the City Drugstore?
   a. a prescription written on a piece of notebook paper
   b. a written prescription covered with coffee stains
   c. a prescription called in by a doctor
   d. a prescription for painkillers with a date showing it was written the day before

48. The owner of the Chevrolet dealership tells Officer Chervenack that sometime after 10:30 P.M. someone is stealing running boards and other parts from the vans he has parked in the south lot. Officer Chervenack decides to patrol the area carefully. Which of the following situations should she investigate?

  a. After midnight, a male in his early twenties is walking up and down rows of new pickups parked near the edge of the dealership.

  b. After midnight, a panel truck pulls out of the vacant lot next to the dealership near where the vans are lined up.

  c. After midnight, two teenagers in baggy pants and T-shirts are rollerblading around the new cars on the lot.

  d. After midnight, a station wagon drives into the lot and stops near the door to the main showroom. A man gets out and unloads a mop, a bucket, and a broom.

49. Winslow Elementary School is having a criminal mischief problem: Windows are being broken at the school between 7:00 P.M. and 6:00 A.M. Officer Link has talked to the school principal and is keeping a closer eye on the school. Which of the following situations should he investigate?

  a. At 1:00 A.M., Officer Link watches a man carrying a grocery sack cut through the schoolyard and come out on the other side of the school grounds. The officer can see a loaf of bread protruding out of the sack.

  b. At 11:00 P.M., a car pulls up in the school parking lot. Officer Link sees the driver turn on the cabin light and unfold a map.

  c. Around 11:30 P.M., Officer Link passes the school and sees two figures come out from behind one of the classroom buildings. They stop when they see him and then start walking, each in a different direction.

  d. At 9:00 P.M., several teenagers skateboard into the parking lot, set up a small wooden ramp, and practice skateboarding tricks.

50. Four people saw Ramirez snatch a woman's purse. Which description of Ramirez is probably correct?

  a. He wore blue pants and an orange sweatshirt.

  b. He wore blue pants and a red sweatshirt.

  c. He wore black pants and an orange sweatshirt.

  d. He wore blue pants and an orange jacket.

Answers

1. d. None of the teams are exempt from traveling to any duty location within the sector. This question is about the canine teams in Agent Smith's sector. According to the last sentence in the paragraph, all the canine teams must be available to travel to any duty station within the sector. This is equivalent to saying that none of the teams are exempt from traveling to any duty location within the sector, choice **d**. Choices **b** and **c** contradict the information in the last sentence. The third sentence in the paragraph informs us that most teams are stationed along the border. Choices **a** and **e** contradict this information.

2. c. If special funding is not needed from the city council, it is not a holiday weekend. Combining the information in the last two sentences, we know that if it is a holiday weekend, special funding is needed from the city council due to assigning additional staff to duty. Accordingly, if special funding is not needed, it must not be a holiday weekend; otherwise, special funding would be needed. Choices **a** and **e** are false because they contradict the information in the paragraph. Choices **b** and **d** might be true, but they are not fully supported by the paragraph.

3. b. All cross-border tunnels are used for narcotics smuggling. This is an example of a test question with a negative lead statement. It asks for the conclusion that is NOT supported by the paragraph. That means that four of the statements are valid conclusions based on the paragraph while one is not. In this case, choice **b** is invalid. The paragraph says that *most* cross-border tunnels are used for smuggling narcotics, but choice **b** says that *all* cross-border tunnels are used for smuggling narcotics. Choice **a** is based on the information that most cross-border tunnels are crudely constructed. Choices **c** and **d** are based on the information that most cross-border tunnels are used to smuggle narcotics. Finally, choice **e** combines all information about the tunnels being crudely constructed and used for smuggling narcotics.

4. a. All of the employees from Honduras were working legally. The correct answer is **a**. The last sentence of the paragraph states that none of the illegal workers were from Honduras, which is equivalent to saying that none of the employees from Honduras were working illegally. Given that none were working illegally, it must be the case that all were working legally. From the information in the paragraph, we know that all the female employees were working legally and that all the employees from Honduras were working legally. However, there is insufficient information to determine if any of the female employees were from Honduras. Therefore, choices **c**, **d**, and **e** cannot be validly concluded. Choice **b** contradicts the information that all the female employees were working legally.

5. c. J.B. was not born in the United States to U.S. citizen parents. According to the paragraph, there are two ways of acquiring U.S. citizenship at birth. Also, the paragraph states that J.B. did not acquire U.S. citizenship at birth. Therefore, the only conclusion that can be validly drawn is that J.B. did not meet either of the two conditions for acquiring U.S. citizenship at birth. Specifically, J.B. was not born in the United States to U.S. citizen parents, and J.B. was not born overseas to U.S. citizen parents who previously lived in the United States for the required period of time. Any other conclusion is not supported by the information in the paragraph.

6. d. If Officer Stoler must physically force entry into the home, then Officer Stoler is not required to ensure that the home is secure upon leaving. This is a negative lead question, so the correct response is the only response option that CANNOT be validly concluded. The first sentence in the paragraph states that when officers must physically force entry into a home, the officers are required to ensure that the home is in a secure condition when they leave. Choice **d** contradicts this information in saying that Officer Stoler is not required to leave the home in a secure condition. Thus, choice **d** is the correct response. Choice **a** is valid and follows from the information in the fourth sentence. Choices **b** and **e** are valid and follow from the information in the first sentence. Choice **c** follows from the information in the second sentence and is valid.

7. d. All the vehicles that did not contain bundles of marijuana were registered. The fourth sentence contains the information that all the unregistered vehicles contained bundles of marijuana. Accordingly, if a vehicle did not contain bundles of marijuana, it could not be one of the unregistered vehicles since all unregistered vehicles contained marijuana. Therefore, it can be deduced that all the vehicles that did not contain bundles of marijuana were registered. Choice **a** contradicts the information in the last sentence. Choice **b** contradicts the information in the fourth sentence. Choice **c** assumes that only unregistered vehicles contained bundles of marijuana, but there is insufficient information to make that conclusion. Choice **e** assumes that some of the registered vehicles also contained bundles of marijuana, but there is insufficient information to make that conclusion.

8. a. H.B.'s departure is not voluntary if H.B.'s passport is allowed to be returned to H.B. This is a negative lead question, so the correct response is the only response option that CANNOT be validly concluded. According to the second sentence, if the alien's departure is voluntary, then the passport is allowed to be returned to the alien. Based on this information, choice **a** is invalid. Choices **c** and **d** are both valid and are supported by the information in the second sentence that the passport is allowed to be returned to H.B. if his departure is voluntary. Choices **b** and **e** are valid and are supported by the information in the first sentence that H.B.'s passport will be returned to the issuing government if H.B. is being removed.

9. b. Few arrestees are able to see after being sprayed with OC. The third sentence says that almost all arrestees are unable to see after being sprayed with OC. Accordingly, few arrestees are able to see after being sprayed with OC, choice **b**. Choice **a** is false because, according to the first sentence, OC is an example of a tool that causes a burning sensation of the eyes but is not deadly force. Sentences four and five do not say that the agencies that have experienced fewer allegations of use of excessive force are the same agencies that have reported a reduction in officer and arrestee injuries; thus, choice **c** is invalid. Choice **d** is false because it contradicts the information in the fourth sentence that some agencies using OC have experienced fewer allegations. Finally, the first sentence states that OC is an effective, non-lethal tool for violent or threatening arrestees, but it does not state that OC is the only tool (choice **e**).

10. a. Inmate Garvey has committed an assault and his behavior is definitely disruptive. Choices **b** and **d** do not warrant that degree of disciplinary intervention. Although some inmates might be sent to solitary for participating in the food fight, choice **a** is a much more obvious choice.

11. b. Vehicles that can easily carry hidden cargo should be searched as a matter of course. Add the fact that the driver is acting oddly, and you have a highly suspicious set of circumstances. Of course, inmates may be able to hide in the vehicles mentioned in the other choices, but this is the most suspicious situation.

12. a. If the officer cannot tell for sure that an inmate is physically present in the bunk, he needs to check more closely. In the other choices, there is clearly a living person present.

13. d. If an officer expects to find weapons and contraband, the searches should be done when inmates are not expecting to be searched. Any kind of warning or set pattern gives the inmates time to find better hiding places or give the contraband to other inmates who aren't expecting to be searched.

14. b. The fight between the two inmates would require documentation, in case disciplinary action is taken and to create a record of inmate behavior. None of the other choices would involve seriously disruptive behavior that would require an officer to make a written record of what has transpired.

15. d. The frequent handshakes are unusual and might indicate that the visitor is passing drugs or other contraband to the inmate.

16. a. Officer Riley needs to talk to inmate Napier if he is to have a chance at heading off a problem. Taking the actions listed in the other choices would postpone the problem rather than trying to solve it.

17. c. Choices **a** and **d** will most likely not result in an accurate count of inmates. Choice **b** may result in too much of a delay if an inmate has escaped during recreational time.

18. d. Not only is calling an inmate's wife every day not within the scope of a correction's officer's duties, but this action could also easily leave the officer open to blackmail. The other situations are normal decisions and requests for officers to consider.

19. c. The text states that Officer Diamond issued 270 summonses, which was ten fewer than Officer Elia. Therefore, Officer Elia issued 280 summonses.

20. c. There is something seriously wrong with a person who can sleep through a police officer trying to wake him or her up. Although the man is likely a drug user, human life always takes precedence over an arrest. After the man receives medical treatment, he may still be arrested. Calling a supervisor (choice **d**) to the scene of any call where an officer should be able to make the decision is not the best option.

21. c. The elements of the license plate number that most often repeat in the eyewitness descriptions are XIW and 017. Therefore, the correct license number is most likely XIW 017.

22. a. The fact that the burglar walked with a limp is the only element of the description likely to remain constant over time and will therefore be most helpful to the police.

23. d. A man walking down the street in the afternoon carrying a television set is the most likely of all the choices to be the daytime burglar, since people do not regularly carry appliances on the street. The teenaged boy is drawing attention to himself and so is unlikely to have stolen the radio. There is also less reason to suspect the woman, who is probably a door-to-door salesperson. It is likely that the man in the car is having a late lunch.

24. d. In all situational questions, human life takes precedence over property. Additionally, any time a police officer pursues a suspect, the officer should be weighing the risks associated with capturing the suspect against the risk to human life, particularly the lives of innocent people. In this instance, the officer's best course of action is to notify dispatch of the fire and the description of the man, and then attempt to wake anyone in the house. If the officer pursues the probable suspect, she puts people who might be asleep in the house at greater risk. Because the officer is not a trained firefighter and the garden hose is not a viable firefighting option, her best course is to attempt to wake the residents, render aid, and then assist in the pursuit of the suspect after the arrival of the fire department.

25. c. Although most silent alarm calls are false, the fact that this one is occurring in an area of predominantly closed manufacturing businesses slightly increases the chances that the alarm is reporting an actual break-in. Therefore, Dodrill should not ignore the call. Because there is nothing in the scenario to indicate that human life is at risk, the use of the emergency lights and siren is inappropriate. Any time an officer uses that equipment, there is an increased risk of causing or becoming involved in a traffic accident.

26. b. Neither choice **a** nor choice **d** is likely to return the money to the rightful owner. More importantly, the money may not have been misplaced; it may have been dropped by one of the prisoners because it is somehow connected to a crime. The best course of action is to complete a report and deposit the money with the department.

27. d. An officer who is looking for auto thieves should pay attention to a man who is trying to open car doors. The transient in choice **a** may be panhandling, but there is no reason to suspect car theft. People often sit on car hoods, as in choice **b**. The man in choice **c** probably owns the vehicle he's standing near.

28. c. The order of seniority would be James, Smyth, Barton, and Ducale.

29. b. Tall, thin, and middle-aged are the elements of the description repeated most often and are therefore most likely to be accurate.

30. d. Sentence 2 in the passage lists several additional beliefs that fall under *attachment to the Constitution* (supporting choice **d**). Choice **a** is ruled out by the final sentence of the passage, which says that an applicant cannot be excluded simply because he or she believes *it might be desirable to make a change in our form of government*. However, it does not say that a person must have a desire to change the government, ruling out choices **b** and **c**. Choice **e** is ruled out by the final sentence of the passage.

31. e. Choice **e** is correct because the passage states in sentence 3 that *some people believe that too much immigration may compromise the standard of living in the United States.* Choice **a** is illogical because its two parts have nothing to do with one another. Choice **b** is illogical, because the chances are good that citizens would not want the United States' standard of living lowered (because it would affect them adversely); therefore, they would tend not to want an open immigration policy. Choice **c** is illogical because what the citizens want has nothing to do with immigration's compromising the United States' standard of living. Choice **d** is incorrect because the historical fact cannot be changed; in addition, the U.S. immigration policy is unrelated to past treatment of people who already lived here.

32. c. This question lists conditions under which visa requests must be refused. Choices **a**, **b**, and **d** are refuted by the third sentence. Choice **e** is incorrect because of the use of the word *among* at the start of the third sentence of the passage.

33. e. Choice **e** is correct because, if the child is considered to have dual nationality, then he must have met the criteria for citizenship in the state in which he was born *and* in his parents' home state—the situation described in choice **e**. Choice **a** is incorrect because in this instance the child cannot be a citizen of the parents' home state and have dual nationality. Choice **b** is incorrect because in this instance, the child cannot be a citizen of the state where he was born. Choice **c** is incorrect because in this instance, the child will be a citizen of the parents' home state and, therefore, will not be stateless. Choice **d** is incorrect because in this instance, the child will be a citizen of his parents' home state.

34. c. Choices **a** and **b** are incorrect because the language in the amendment says that states cannot abridge the privileges of their citizens without due process. Choice **d** is incorrect because the amendment does differentiate between *citizens* and *any person*. Choice **e** is refuted by the last part of the passage.

35. b. Choice **b** includes the following premises: People are accountable for their own behavior, and people are not accountable for behavior they cannot control. The logical conclusion based on these premises is that people can control their own behavior. Choice **a** would require that criminals never have control over the behavior of other people, which the argument does not prove. Choice **c** requires that people should not be held accountable for the behavior of other people. Choice **d** is not a conclusion, as it simply reiterates a premise of the argument. Choice **e** provides for the possibility that a criminal might not have control over another person's behavior, which is subject to harsh criminal sentencing.

36. b. Choice **b** is supported by the fact that, in *Matter of Kohama*, the relatives submitted evidence that they were willing and able to support the couple, and the court accepted the evidence as sufficient. The example in the passage is of relatives who lived in the United States; the passage does not discuss people with relatives in their home country (ruling out choice **a**). Choice **c** is illogical because of the word *must*—the relatives cannot force the person to immigrate. The passage simply states that aliens will be excluded if they are likely to become a public charge—there are obviously other ways to avoid becoming a public charge (such as employment), ruling out choice **e**.

37. e. Each of the other choices draws conclusions about the relative importance of activities either at the border or away from the border that cannot be validly concluded from the paragraph.

38. c. Choices **a**, **b**, and **e** are incorrect because they make assumptions about the relationship between terrorists and illegal aliens not supported by the passage. Choices **a** and **b** make assumptions possible for *some* incorrect by stating them for *all*. Choices **d** and **e** might sometimes be true, but are unsupported by the passage.

39. d. Choice **d** focuses on the combination of solutions outlined in the passage. All the other choices make assumptions about individual solutions that are not supported by the passage.

40. e. Choice **e** is correct because it is directly supported by the second sentence and the last sentence in the paragraph. The information in choice **a** is specifically contradicted by the first sentence. Choices **b** and **c** are incorrect because there are no supporting statements in the paragraph. Choice **d** is incorrect because the passage clearly states that agency regulations and directives provide field-level guidance to agents and that the judicial branch of government interprets statutory law.

41. e. In choice **a**, the word *always* is not supported by the paragraph. Choices **b**, **c**, and **d** draw conclusions about the value of technology that are not supported by the information in the paragraph.

42. c. Choice **c** is the only statement that can be validly concluded directly from the information in the question. The statements made in answers **a**, **b**, **d**, and **e** use the words *never* and *always* to make assertions that are not supported by the paragraph.

43. b. Choice **b** accurately reflects the third sentence of the passage. The small word *unless* rules out choice **a**. Choices **c**, **d**, and **e** all erroneously apply the criteria for *becoming exempt* from the literacy requirements to *meeting* the literacy requirements.

44. a. The question asks that you identify what is NOT in the passage. Because the search-and-rescue dogs are labeled disobedient, and only *some* (not all) of the precincts have search-and-rescue dogs, it is *not* true that all precincts have disobedient dogs (supporting choice **a**). The other choices can be found in the passage and are therefore incorrect answers to this *cannot* question.

45. b. The second sentence says that a child is an orphan if her parents have disappeared or abandoned her, suggesting that the parents may still be alive. Choice **a** is wrong, because one of the conditions specified in the second sentence is that, in order to be considered an orphan, the parents must have *irrevocably released the child for emigration and adoption*. Choices **c** and **d** are irrelevant to the matter of who is an orphan, because both answers, instead, explain how an orphan can be adopted. Choice **e** is ruled out by the second sentence, which lists ways a child can become an orphan, even if the parents are still alive.

46. d. Seeing a man running through the vacant lot with a bulky item under his shirt should make the officer suspicious. A purse snatcher would very likely choose to run through the vacant lot to get away from the area and would want to hide an object as obvious as a stolen purse from view. Choice **a** is not particularly suspicious, given that most car alarms activate the car horn and that car alarms frequently go off in parking lots. In choice **b**, a car with flat tires and a broken windshield may indicate criminal mischief, but it isn't necessarily linked to the purse snatchings. In choice **c**, a woman's voice raised in anger would be a plausible thing to hear following a purse snatching, but it's not nearly as suspicious as the situation in choice **d**.

47. a. Prescriptions are usually written on standardized prescription pads recognized by pharmacists. A prescription written on any other kind of paper would be suspect. In choice **b**, the doctor or the patient could be responsible for the coffee stains. It has no apparent bearing on the validity of the prescription. Choice **c** is incorrect because doctors frequently phone in prescriptions. In choice **d**, it may be odd that the patient is just now getting around to filling a prescription for painkillers, but the fact that it took a day to do so does not necessarily suggest forgery.

48. b. A panel truck pulling out of a vacant lot near a car dealership that has suffered a rash of thefts of auto parts is suspicious. The truck would be able to hold plenty of auto parts. The two rollerbladers in choice **c** aren't likely to be able to carry off a new running board without attracting attention. The male in his early twenties in choice **a** appears to be doing what a lot of people do at night, which is look at new cars without having to worry about sales personnel. It is not unusual for cleanup crews to arrive late at night after everyone has gone, as in choice **d**.

49. c. The odd behavior and the location of the two figures should cause the officer to investigate, given the problems the school has been having.

50. a. Blue pants, sweatshirt, and the color orange are the elements repeated most often by the eyewitnesses and are therefore most likely correct.

SKILL BUILDING UNTIL NEXT TIME

Analyze how you performed on the practice questions. Did you get any particular questions wrong? Is there a pattern to what you had trouble with? If so, attempt to ascertain where you

11 ▶ Logical Fallacies: Appeals to Emotion

LESSON SUMMARY

Arguments that appeal to people's emotions rather than to their sense of logic and reason abound in everyday life. In this lesson, you'll learn how to recognize several common appeals to emotion so that you can make more informed and logical decisions.

You are a police officer assigned to traffic enforcement. You pull over a car that just went through a red light. You get out of your patrol car and approach the driver and ask for her license and registration. The driver looks at you and says, "Officer, that light was yellow. It was not red. If you give me a ticket, I'm going to make a formal complaint about you!" Obviously, this driver is attempting to get out of the ticket. The driver is trying to avoid the ticket not by arguing with any *reason* or *logic*, but by manipulating your *emotions*.

People will use many strategies to try to convince you that their conclusions are sound. Unfortunately, many of these strategies *appear* to be logical when, in fact, they're not. These strategies—often called **logical fallacies** or **pseudo reasoning** (false reasoning)—can lead you to make poor decisions and accept arguments that really don't hold water. That's why the next three lessons cover some of the most common logical fallacies. The more of them you can recognize—and the more you can avoid them in your own arguments—the better problem solver and decision maker you will be.

This lesson addresses four fallacies that appeal to your emotions rather than to your sense of reason: scare tactics, flattery, peer pressure, and appeals to pity.

Scare Tactics

In the opening scenario, the driver attempted to avoid receiving a traffic summons by playing to your emotions. The driver threatened to make a formal complaint about you. She used a threat to prod you into accepting her conclusion (that she should not receive a summons). She didn't provide you with any logical reasons for not issuing her a summons; instead, she played upon your emotions. She used a logical fallacy known as *scare tactics*.

Scare tactics are used very commonly in deductive arguments, and they can be quite powerful. Although sometimes scare tactics cross the line and can become very real threats to your physical or emotional well-being, in most cases, you're not in any real danger. Once you know what to look for, you can see right through scare tactics. For example, read the following argument:

> Support Governor Wilson, or your children will receive a poor public school education.

Sounds convincing, doesn't it? After all, who wants their children to receive a poor education? But is this a good argument? Notice that the only reason this argument gives you for supporting the conclusion is emotional. It aims to frighten you into supporting Governor Wilson. The argument would be much more powerful if it also provided a logical reason for your support.

Practice

Read the following arguments carefully. If the argument uses logic to support the conclusion, write an **L** in the blank. If the argument uses scare tactics, write an **S** in the blank.

_____ **1.** We'd better leave the park now. If we don't, we can be locked in when they close the gates.

_____ **2.** I really think it would be a good idea to do whatever she asks. She's a pretty powerful person.

_____ **3.** I really think it's a good idea to do whatever he asks. I've seen him fire people who say no to him.

Answers

1. **L.** The reasons given appeal to common sense.
2. **S.** This argument suggests that she is a person who can hurt you if you don't do what she wants.
3. **S.** This item may have tricked you, because it seems like this reason could be logical. But just because the arguer has seen this person fire others doesn't provide you with logical reasons for doing "whatever he asks." Who knows—what he asks of you could be illegal or dangerous. This person is trying to scare you into doing what he wants.

Flattery

They say flattery will get you nowhere, but they're wrong. Flattery is powerful. So powerful, in fact, that it often leads people to make poor decisions and to accept arguments that really have no logical basis. Just as people can appeal to the sense of fear, they can also appeal to our **vanity**, which is another logical fallacy. Here's an example:

> "Officer, you seem like a kind and considerate person. You would not give an elderly woman a ticket, would you?"

Notice that this argument doesn't give you any logical reasons for not giving the woman a traffic ticket. Instead, it flatters you; you like hearing that you are a kind and considerate person. While this may be true about you, is that any reason to not issue a summons when it is warranted? No. This argument doesn't give any plausible reason for committing a traffic violation. Here's another example of an appeal to vanity:

> "C.O. Smith, you are the fairest corrections officer in this place. You treat us like human beings and you are smarter than all these other guys in here. You should run this place. Would you be able to give me a little bit longer visitation time this week with my family?"

Here, the prisoner doesn't give the corrections officer any reason to make an exception to the visitation policy. The C.O. may indeed be fair and smart, but the prisoner is not giving any good reasons for extended visitation; he's just buttering up the C.O. to get him to say yes.

Practice

Read the following arguments carefully. Are they using logic (**L**) or appealing to vanity (**V**)?

_____ **4.** Teacher to class: "This has been the best class I've ever taught. You're always so prepared and eager to learn! Thank you all so much. Now, I have these end-of-the-semester evaluations I need you to fill out. I know you'll all be honest and fill them out carefully. Thank you."

_____ **5.** "Claire, I'd like you to handle this typing project. You're the fastest typist and the best at reading my handwriting."

_____ **6.** "Claire, I know you don't mind a little extra work—you're such a good sport! So I'd like you to handle this typing project. You're the best. By the way, that's a terrific outfit."

Answers

4. V. This is a definite appeal to the students' vanity. The teacher is hoping that by buttering the students up a bit—telling them how wonderful they are—they'll be more generous in their evaluations of the class.

5. L. The speaker provides two logical, practical reasons for Claire to handle the project.

6. V. The speaker is trying to convince Claire she should do the extra work by flattering her. Notice that none of the reasons directly relates to her ability to do the work well.

Peer Pressure

Along with fear and vanity, another extremely powerful emotion is our desire to be accepted by others. For example, children often do things they know are wrong because of pressure from friends. Unfortunately, many people continue to give in to peer pressure throughout their lives. **Peer pressure** is another form of false reasoning. It is an argument that says, "Accept the conclusion, or _you_ won't be accepted." Take a look at the following arguments for examples of peer pressure:

> "C'mon, Sally. Stay. Everyone else is."
> "We're all voting _no_, Joe. You should, too."

In both these examples, the arguers don't offer any logical reasons for accepting their conclusions. Instead, they offer you acceptance—you'll be like everyone else. It's the old "everyone else is doing it" argument. The counterargument is exactly the one your mother gave you: If everyone else were jumping off a cliff, would you do it, too?

No one likes to be left out, and that's why we often give in to peer pressure. It *is* hard to be different and stand alone. But it is important to remember that our desire to belong is *not* a logical reason for accepting an argument. *Why* should Joe vote *no*? He needs to hear some specific, logical reasons. Otherwise, he's just falling victim to false logic.

Practice

Read the following arguments carefully. Are the arguers using logic (**L**) or peer pressure (**P**) to try to convince you?

_____ **7.** "*We* all think that the death penalty is the only way to cure society of rampant crime. Don't you?"

_____ **8.** "Come on, we're all voting for the Democrat again, just like the last time."

_____ **9.** "Stick with your party, Joe. The more unified we are, the more likely our candidates will win."

_____ **10.** "You should stop eating red meat. We've stopped and we feel much healthier."

Answers

7. P. The speaker tries to get you to agree by stressing that everyone else thinks that way. He suggests that if you disagree, you'll be alone in your belief.

8. P. Again, the speaker is using peer pressure. Here, the suggestion is that everyone else is voting the same way, so you should, too. But the speaker doesn't provide any logical reasons for voting for the Democrat.

9. L. This time, the speaker gives Joe a good logical reason for voting along the party line: Their party's candidates will win.

10. L. The speaker gives a good reason for considering his or her claim: They feel much better since they've stopped eating red meat. Of course, you'd probably want to hear more supporting arguments before you decide, but this argument doesn't try to sway you with emotion.

Pity

Mr. Jones, a probation officer, is making a field visit to Harry. Harry is on probation for a drug arrest and as a condition of his probation, he must be clean of drugs and alcohol. Mr. Jones goes to Harry's house and finds Harry drinking a beer. Harry tells the probation officer, "It's my birthday. I was just having one beer to celebrate turning forty. I'm sorry and I won't do it again. Please don't send me back to prison for one beer. My wife and kids will be devastated." What should Mr. Jones do?

- violate Harry and send him back to prison
- give Harry a warning

Mr. Jones more than likely should give Harry a break. But are the reasons Harry offered sufficient to warrant leniency? No. Harry knows the rules of his probation and he must follow them. If he does not, he should be sent back to prison. What Harry is offering is an appeal to another one of the most powerful emotions—the sense of pity and compassion for others. No one wants to be seen as heartless or uncaring. And that's why the appeal to pity, another logical fallacy, often works.

Here's another example of an appeal to pity:

Support salary increases for your local police officers. They work in a very dangerous environment, keeping you and your family safe at night. Their job is very dangerous and often thankless. Give them raises.

Notice that this argument asks the listener to support a cause purely for *emotional* reasons. It appeals to the sense of compassion for hardworking police officers. While this may be a compelling argument—after all, these people do deserve compassion—it is not a *logical* one. It doesn't directly address *why* increasing salaries for police officers is a reasonable policy.

Of course, you will have to judge each situation individually. But just as with the other appeals to emotion, it's important to have some logical reasons to balance the emotional. Unfortunately, if decisions are made based purely on pity, they often come back to haunt you. There are some people in the world who will take advantage of your sense of compassion, so think carefully before you act on pity alone.

Practice

Read the following arguments carefully. Are they using logic (**L**) to convince you, or are they appealing to your sense of pity and compassion (**P**)?

____ **11.** "You can't arrest me. It's Christmas."

____ **12.** "You can't arrest me. I did not break that guy's window. Besides, it Christmas and I have to get home to see my kids!"

____ **13.** "You can't arrest me. I'm starving and all I did was ask people for money to buy some food."

Answers

11. P. The only reason the speaker gives for not being arrested is that it is Christmas. He doesn't make any argument regarding whether he committed the crime.

12. L. And a little pity. The speaker offers a logical reason for not arresting him as well as an emotional one.

13. P. However, as always, you need to consider each case individually. Maybe the speaker is really hungry and just trying to get some food. In that case, it might be okay to be swayed a little by pity.

In Short

Appeals to emotions, including fear, vanity, desire to belong, and pity, can be very powerful. It is important to recognize when an argument uses emotional appeals—especially when emotional appeals are the only kind of support the argument offers. Law enforcement officers must be careful not to play into appeals to emotions. It may hinder their abilities to fully interpret evidence and testimony and resolve situations properly.

SKILL BUILDING UNTIL NEXT TIME

- Listen carefully for emotional appeals throughout the day. If you like to watch television, you'll see that these appeals are very often used in sitcoms.
- Think about something that you want someone to do for you. Think of several good, logical reasons for that person to say yes. Then, think of four different emotional appeals—one from each category—that you might use if you didn't know better.

 12 ▶ Logical Fallacies: The Impostors

LESSON SUMMARY

Some forms of logical fallacies are tougher to recognize than others because they *seem* logical. This lesson helps you spot several common fallacies, including *circular reasoning* and *two wrongs make a right*.

"Either you're with us or you're against us. Which is it?" Have you ever been put on the spot like this before, where you were forced to decide between two contradictory options? Chances are you have. But chances are you also had more choices than you thought.

Logical fallacies come in many forms. The previous lesson covered the false reasoning that appeals to your emotions rather than to your sense of logic. This lesson examines four logical fallacies that are sometimes a little harder to detect because they don't appeal to your emotions. As a result, they may *seem* logical even though they aren't. These types of fallacies are called **impostors**. Four types are covered in this lesson, including *no in-betweens*, *slippery slope*, *circular reasoning*, and *two wrongs make a right*.

No In-Betweens

No in-betweens (also called *false dilemma*) is a logical fallacy that aims to convince you that there are only two choices: *X* and *Y*, and nothing in between. The so-called logic behind this fallacy is that if you think there are only two choices, then you won't stop to consider other possibilities. The arguer hopes that you will therefore be more likely to accept his or her conclusion. Law enforcement officers utilize this type of reasoning often, as it is very compelling.

For example, have you ever heard a police officer say, "Either you leave or you are going to get arrested"? The officer obviously wants the person to leave, so he or she presents the person with two extremes, go away or get arrested. When given these options, very few people will say, "Arrest me." In reality, there are numerous other options that can satisfy both the police officer and the person he is dealing with. It is important to remember that there are very few situations in which there are only two options. There are almost always other choices.

Practice

1. Let's practice using the preceding scenario. What other options are available?

   Either you leave or you are going to get arrested.

Answer

There are plenty of other options. You could stay and stop causing a problem or you could take a walk to blow off some steam for a little while and return when you are calm. Perhaps the officer could give you a ride to a friend or relatives' house. Maybe you could just stay and go to bed. In other words, there are plenty of in-betweens here.

Practice

Read the following arguments carefully. Do the arguers use logic (**L**) or no in-betweens (**NI**) to convince you?

_____ **2.** He is either guilty or innocent.

_____ **3.** We can go to the movies or to the bowling alley. Unfortunately, because of the holiday, everything else is closed.

_____ **4.** Either you get tough with the prisoners or they don't respect you.

_____ **5.** Either you get tough on crime or you let crime go through the roof.

Answers

2. **NI.** The subject may not have committed the crime, but he could have been an accessory after the fact. In this case he would not be guilty, but also not completely innocent.
3. **L.** If everything else is closed, then these really are the only two options available.
4. **NI.** There are definitely other choices. You can treat the prisoners fairly, respectfully, and equally. Getting tough is not the only way to earn respect.
5. **NI.** You can be in-between on this issue. For example, you can be against the death penalty and also tough on crime.

Slippery Slope

We need to secure our borders. If we don't, the next thing you know, crime in this country will be out of control.

Right?

Well, maybe, but probably not and definitely not for certain. This type of logical fallacy—often called **slippery slope**—presents an if/then scenario. It argues that if *X* happens, then *Y* will follow. This "next thing you know" argument has one major flaw, however: *X* doesn't necessarily lead to *Y*. When you hear someone make a claim in this format, you need to use your critical thinking and reasoning skills. You need to carefully consider whether there's a logical relationship between *X* and *Y*. If we don't secure our borders, for example, does that *necessarily* mean that crime will dramatically increase? Definitely not.

First of all, no connection has been found between immigrants and crime. Second, the majority of crimes in this country are committed by non-immigrants. And third, nearly half of all illegal immigrants in the United States enter the country legally. So, though the thought of uncontrolled immigration may be frightening, it's not logical to severely restrict it because we're afraid of crime. More logical reasons need to be presented to justify this type of policy.

Practice

Read the following arguments carefully. Are they using logic (**L**) or slippery slope (**SS**) to convince you?

_____ **6.** If we raise the legal driving age to 18, there will be less car accidents on the roads. People will feel safer on the road, and car insurance rates for everyone will decrease significantly.

_____ **7.** If all employers required their employees to take a flu shot, less people would take sick days. This would result in increased productivity for the nation as a whole.

_____ **8.** If we collect everyone's DNA at birth, we can solve more crimes.

Answers

6. SS. Raising the driving age to 18 does not necessarily mean that there would be less car accidents on the roads. First of all, we can't be sure that the majority of car accidents that take place involve drivers under 18. Second, even if there were less car accidents as a result of the new driving age, it wouldn't necessarily result in lower insurance rates for everyone.

7. SS. Again, *X* doesn't necessarily lead to *Y*. There's no reason to believe that taking flu shots will increase productivity. Also, people can get sick for other reasons, and flu shots might not help in those cases.

8. L. This is a good, logical reason to collect everyone's DNA at birth.

Circular Reasoning

You have identified a suspect in an arson case and bring him in for an interview. At one point during the interview, you look him straight in the eyes and say, "Did you set fire to this house?"

The subject looks at you and says, "I didn't set fire to this." You then ask why you should believe him and he says, "Because I don't light fires."

The suspect has just committed a very common logical fallacy called **circular reasoning** (also known as *begging the question*). Circular reasoning is a very appropriate name, because that's what this false logic does: It goes in a circle. Notice how the subject's argument doubles back on itself. In other words, his conclusion and premise say essentially the same thing:

Conclusion: "I didn't set fire to this house."
Premise: "I don't light fires."

Instead of progressing logically from conclusion to evidence, the argument gets stuck at the conclusion. Like a dog chasing its tail, it goes nowhere. Here's another example:

"You know that's not good for you; it isn't healthy."

Notice how the premise "it isn't healthy" is no support for the conclusion, "that's not good for you"—rather, it simply restates it. Again, the argument goes nowhere.

Circular reasoning can be particularly tricky because a conclusion that doubles back on itself often *sounds* strong. That is, by restating the conclusion, you reinforce the idea that you're trying to convey. But you're *not* offering any logical reasons to accept that argument. When you hear someone make a claim that follows this format, look for a logical premise to support the conclusion—you probably won't find one.

Practice

See if you can recognize circular reasoning in the following arguments. If the argument is logical, write an **L** in the blank. If the argument is circular, write a **C** in the blank.

____ **9.** I know he's telling the truth because he's not lying.

____ **10.** He is not guilty because he is innocent.

____ **11.** He is not guilty because he has a solid alibi.

____ **12.** It's the right thing to do, because this way, no one will get hurt.

____ **13.** We believe this is the best choice because it's the right thing to do.

Answers

9. C. This argument doubles back on itself— "he's not lying" doesn't say any more than what's already been said in the conclusion.

10. C. Notice that the premise doesn't give any reason for the subject not being guilty Not guilty and innocent are the same thing.

11. L. The premise here offers a real reason. He has a solid alibi, therefore he could not have committed the crime.

12. L. Preventing people from getting hurt is a good supporting premise for the conclusion here.

13. C. Unlike number 12, the premise and the conclusion here say essentially the same thing.

Two Wrongs Make a Right

Two prisoners get into a fight in the mess hall. You are in charge of the disciplinary investigation and you interview one of the prisoners. You ask him to explain his actions.

He tells you, "I heard that he was going to hit me so I hit him first. I thought that he wanted to fight me."

The reasons given by the prisoner for his actions may seem to be logical, but, as with the other fallacies, it's not—the conclusion he draws doesn't come from good reasoning. He has fallen victim to the two wrongs make a right fallacy.

The **two wrongs make a right** fallacy assumes that it's okay for you to do something to someone else because someone else *might* do that same thing to you. But two wrongs *don't* make a right, especially when you're talking about *mights*. If one prisoner is afraid that another will punch him, does that make it all right to hit him first? Of course not.

Don't get this fallacy confused with the *eye for an eye* mentality. The *two wrongs* logical fallacy is not about getting even. It's about getting an edge. In an eye for an eye, you do something to someone because that person has *already* done it to you. But two wrongs make a right argues that you can do something simply because someone else *might* do it to you. And that's neither logical nor fair.

To show you how illogical this fallacy is, imagine the following scenario. You are walking home alone late at night. As you turn onto your street, you notice a man walking toward you. Although he gives no indication that he has any bad intentions, you clutch the canister of mace in your pocket. Just as you are about to cross paths, you decide—just to be on the safe side—to spray this stranger in the eyes. After all, you think, "What if he was planning to mug me? I'd better get him first."

As you can see, this approach is neither logical nor fair. It can also create a dangerous situation out of a perfectly normal one. Two wrongs that are built on a *maybe*—even a *probably*—don't make a right.

Practice

14. Put a check mark next to the arguments below that use the two wrongs make a right fallacy.
  a. I ran away from home because they were probably going to punish me.
  b. I scratched her car with a key because she did the same thing to my car last week.
  c. We beat him up because we heard that he was coming after us.

Answer

Arguments **a** and **c** use the two wrongs make a right fallacy. Argument **b** may look like it does, but look again. In this case, the arguer is saying that he damaged her car in retaliation. This is truly an eye for an eye, not an eye for a maybe.

In Short

Logical fallacies can appear to be logical; to avoid falling into their traps, you need to be on the lookout for false reasoning. The **no in-betweens** fallacy tries to convince you that there are only two choices, when in reality there are many options. The **slippery slope** fallacy tries to convince you that if you do X, then Y will follow—but in reality, X doesn't necessarily lead to Y. **Circular reasoning** is an argument that goes in a circle—the conclusion and premise say essentially the same thing. Finally, **two wrongs make a right** claims that it is okay to do something to someone else because someone else might do that same thing to you.

SKILL BUILDING UNTIL NEXT TIME

- Each of the logical fallacies discussed in this lesson is very common. Listen for them throughout the day. Again, these fallacies are the kind you might see in various sitcoms, so look for them even when you're watching television.
- Think about something that you want someone to do for you. Come up with reasons based on the logical fallacies you learned in this lesson for that person to say yes. Then think of several good, logical reasons. Those are the reasons you should use when trying to convince someone of something.

L E S S O N

13 ▶ Logical Fallacies: Distracters and Distorters

LESSON SUMMARY

In this final lesson about logical fallacies in deductive reasoning, you'll learn about fallacies that try to divert your attention from the main issue or to distort the issue so you're more likely to accept the argument. These fallacies include *ad hominem*, the *red herring*, and the *straw man*.

It is your first day on the job as a border patrol agent. You are a little nervous and some of the more seasoned agents notice it. Jon, one of the more experienced agents, tells you, "You shouldn't be nervous, you seem like you have a good head on your shoulders. Just relax and learn everything you can. If you have any questions, just ask." Another agent, Frank, sees this and comes up to you and says, "Whatever you do, don't listen to him." He has three open complaints against him. Who do you trust? Who is more credible? You can't answer these questions because you are new to the job, but it is important that you realize that Frank has committed a logical fallacy. In this last lesson about logical fallacies in deductive reasoning, you'll learn about **distracters** and **distorters**—fallacies that aim to confuse the issues so that you more easily accept the conclusion of the argument. *Ad hominem* will be discussed first, followed by red herrings and the straw man.

Ad Hominem

What has Frank done wrong? Indeed, since Jon has three open complaints, how *can* he give you good advice? It would appear as if what Frank says makes a lot of sense.

Frank's argument may seem logical, but it's not. That's because Frank is not attacking Jon's *advice*; instead, he's simply attacking *Jon*. This kind of false reasoning is called **ad hominem**, which in Latin means, "to the man." *Ad hominem* fallacies attack the *person* making the claim rather than the *claim* itself.

An *ad hominem* fallacy can take a variety of forms. You can attack a person, as Frank does, for his or her personality or actions. You can also attack a person for his or her beliefs or affiliations. For example, you might say, "Don't listen to him. He's a liberal." Or you can attack a person for his or her nationality, ethnicity, appearance, occupation, or any other categorization. For example, imagine someone says to you:

> "Of course he's wrong. Someone who dresses like that obviously doesn't have a clue about anything."

This is a clear-cut case of *ad hominem*.

Ad hominem aims to distract you from looking at the validity of the claim by destroying the credibility of the person making the claim. But the trouble with *ad hominem* is that it doesn't really take into account the issue of credibility. Just because Jon has three open complaints doesn't mean he can't give you good advice about how to deal with your first day on the job. In fact, because he's experienced and has dealt with some serious issues such as complaints, he might be considered more of an expert than most. It all depends on what kind of advice you're looking for. Maybe Jon was falsely accused and the complaints will ultimately be dropped. Whatever the case, Jon

may still be in a position to give you good advice. If Frank wants to prove his point, he needs to attack Jon's actual *argument* about how to handle your first day on the job.

To clarify when something is and isn't an *ad hominem*, read the following example:

> Don't take that lawyer's legal advice. He is sneaky.
>
> I wouldn't take that lawyer's legal advice. He is being sued for malpractice and is about to be disbarred.

Are either of these *ad hominem* fallacies? Both? Neither?

You probably saw that the first argument uses *ad hominem*. The lawyer may indeed be sneaky, but that doesn't mean that his legal advice is bad. Whether you *like* him or not is a separate matter from whether he has good advice or not. His "sneaky" nature should not really affect the credibility of his advice. Remember, credibility is based on freedom from bias and on expertise—not on appearance, personality, past behavior, or beliefs.

If, however, the lawyer has recently lost numerous cases, his expertise in the matter of the law should be called into question. He has experience in legal matters, yes—but his experience shows that he may not be too knowledgeable about the subject. You should probably investigate further before deciding whether to listen to his advice. At any rate, at least the second argument avoids the *ad hominem* fallacy.

Ad hominem fallacies can also work in reverse. That is, the argument can urge you to *accept* someone's argument based on who or what the person is rather than on the validity of the premises. For example: Len says, "I agree with Rich. After all, he's a Lithuanian, too." Does the fact that Len and Rich share the same nationality mean that Rich's argument—whatever it may be—is valid? Of course not.

Practice

Read the following arguments carefully. Do they use the *ad hominem* fallacy?

1. Well, if that's what Harvey said, then it must be true.

2. Well, he's got 20 years of experience dealing with consumer complaints, so I think we should trust his advice.

3. He's good, but he's just not right for the job. After all, he's a Jets fan!

4. Police Supervisor A to Supervisor B: "I know we need to address the problem. But Officer Smith doesn't know what she's talking about. She's just a patrol officer."

Answers

1. **Yes.**
2. **No.** His experience makes him credible, and that's a good reason to trust his advice.
3. **Yes.**
4. **Yes.** Just because she's a patrol officer and not a supervisor doesn't mean she doesn't have a good perspective on the problem. In fact, because she's in the trenches, Officer Smith's ideas are probably very valuable to the supervisors.

Red Herring

Just what is a **red herring**? Strange name for a logical fallacy, isn't it? But the name makes sense. Cured red herrings were previously used to throw dogs off the track of an animal they were chasing. And that's ex-

actly what a *red herring* does in an argument: It takes you off the track of the argument by bringing in an unrelated topic to divert your attention from the real issue. Here's an example:

> Prisoners should be given an extra hour each day in the yard. The food really stinks in this facility and the guards are mean.

First, break down the argument. What's the conclusion?

Conclusion: Prisoners should be given an extra hour each day in the yard. Now, what are the premises?

Premises:
1. The food really stinks in this facility.
2. The guards are mean.

Do the premises have anything to do with the conclusion? In fact, do these premises have anything to do with each other? No. Instead of supporting the conclusion, the premises aim to sidetrack you by bringing up at least two new issues:

1. The food really stinks in this facility.
2. The guards are mean.

Red herrings like these can be so distracting that you forget to look for support for the conclusion that the arguer presents. Instead of wondering why the prisoners deserve an extra hour in the yard, you may find yourself thinking about the food and the guards' behavior. If you agree that the food stinks, you may be falsely swayed into supporting the conclusion. Red herrings are a favorite of politicians and people who want to turn potential negative attention away from them and onto others. Watch how it works:

> **Senator Wolf:** "Yes, I support Social Security reform. I know that Senator Fox is against it, but he's just trying to get the liberal vote."

Notice how Senator Wolf avoids having to explain or defend his position by shifting the attention away from his claim and onto Senator Fox. Instead of supporting his claim, he leaves the listener wondering if Senator Fox is just out to get more votes. Once again, the red herring tactic throws the argument off track.

Practice

Read the following arguments carefully. Do you see any red herrings? If so, underline them.

5. Yes, I believe that it is time for rent laws to change, and here's why. It's very hard to pay my rent since my income is so low. How would you feel if you worked 40 hours a week and could barely make ends meet? It's time for a change!

6. It is wrong to censor the press. Our government has a law in the First Amendment that allows the press to express itself without interference or constraint by the government.

7. Do you want to know why crime is out of control? It's because we don't pay our law enforcement officers enough.

8. Marijuana should be legalized. People with cancer are in pain.

Answers

5. Yes, I believe that it is time for rent laws to change, and here's why. <u>It's very hard to pay my rent since my income is so low. How would you feel if you worked 40 hours a week and could barely make ends meet? It's time for a change!</u>

6. It is wrong to censor the press. Our government has a law in the First Amendment that allows the press to express itself without interference or constraint by the government. (This argument provides relevant evidence for the conclusion.)

7. Do you want to know why crime is out of control? <u>It's because we don't pay our law enforcement officers enough.</u>

8. Marijuana should be legalized. <u>People with cancer are in pain.</u>

Straw Man

Have you ever been in a fight with a scarecrow? It's pretty easy to win, isn't it, when you're fighting a man made of straw. After all, he's not a real man—he falls apart easily and he can't fight back. You're safe and your opponent is a goner. It probably doesn't surprise you that there's a logical fallacy that uses this principle: It sets up the opponent as a straw man, making it easy to knock him down.

Specifically, the **straw man** fallacy takes the opponent's position and distorts it. The position can be oversimplified, exaggerated, or otherwise misrepresented. For example, if someone were arguing against the legalization of drugs, he or she might distort the reformers' position by saying:

> "The people who support legalizing drugs are only out to get high and support their own habits."

Even if getting drugs is one of the reasons people support drug reform, it can't be the only one—after all, the legalization of drugs is a pretty complicated issue. Furthermore, the arguer, using the straw man tactic, presents the reformers as selfish, greedy drug addicts which makes it easier for the listeners not to want to support their position.

Similarly, if someone were arguing *for* the legalization of drugs, he or she might set up a straw man like the following:

> "The folks who oppose the legalization of drugs simply are probably the ones profiting from their illegal sale."

True, those making a profit by selling illegal drugs may not want them legalized and controlled, but is that the case for everyone? Is that the real reason they don't support it? Chances are, their opposition stems from a number of issues, of which this is just one. Once again, the straw man has misrepresented and oversimplified, making the opponent easy to knock down. In both cases, the reasons for support or opposition are difficult to approve of. One argument claims that the supporters are selfish drug addicts and the other claims that the opponents are profiting from drugs—and neither of these is an admirable position.

Straw men are very commonly used in arguments because people often don't take the time to consider all sides of an issue or because they don't have the courage or counterarguments to address the complete issue. For example, imagine that someone says:

> "Those environmentalists! They're all trying to make us spend more money on electric automobiles instead of letting us continue to drive gas-powered ones."

Clearly, this is a misinterpreted "definition" of environmentalists. Indeed, it's difficult to sum up what environmentalists—or any group—believe in just one sentence. But if you present environmentalists this way, it becomes very easy to avoid coming up with effective counterarguments, and it certainly becomes difficult to say that environmentalism is a positive thing.

The trouble is, how do you know if you're being presented with a straw man? What if you've never studied environmentalism or don't know much about the environmentalist movement? What if you haven't paid much attention to the news about the legalization of drugs? In short, how do you know when an opponent is being misrepresented?

Your best bet is to be as informed and educated as possible. And you can do that by reading and listening as much as possible. Watch the news, read the paper, listen to the radio, read magazines—pay attention to things like politics and social issues. The more informed you are, the better you'll be able to see if and when someone is trying to pull the wool over your eyes with a straw man.

Practice

Do any of the following arguments use a straw man?

9. All the union members want is to put us middle managers out of work.

10. Lawyers don't really care about helping people. They're just out to make as much money as they can.

11. LeeAnne feels that it's unwise for prisoners to have their own lounge because it reduces guards' view of them and increases the risk for illicit activity.

Answers

9. Yes. The middle managers misrepresent the position of the union members.

10. Yes. This argument makes a sweeping generalization that misrepresents the position of all lawyers.

11. No. This argument makes sense—LeeAnne's position is specific and clear.

In Short

Now you're armed with three more fallacies to watch out for: ***ad hominem***, the **red herring**, and the **straw man**. In *ad hominem*, the arguer attacks the *person* instead of the claim. A *red herring* brings in an irrelevant issue to throw the argument off track. The *straw man* presents a distorted picture of the opponent so that the opponent will be easy to knock down. Be on the lookout for these and the other fallacies you've learned as you assess the validity of arguments.

SKILL BUILDING UNTIL NEXT TIME

- One way to recognize these fallacies is to be sure you can commit them yourself. So, as you did in the previous two lessons, think of several good, logical reasons to support an argument. Then, come up with examples of each of the logical fallacies you learned in this lesson.
- Listen to a call-in talk show on the radio or watch a debate on television, preferably one where audience members are allowed to participate. Listen carefully for the logical fallacies that you've learned. Chances are, you'll catch a lot of people trying to get away with false logic.

14 ▶ Making Judgment Calls

LESSON SUMMARY

Most of the skills that have been explored in this book have had to do with gathering facts and making decisions based on them. Although not always easy, the process is pretty clear-cut: You come to understand the situation you face, learn all you can about it and the options available, and choose a solution. Judgment calls are trickier. You can't collect all the information you need to make a decision, because it does not exist. Even worse, judgment calls typically need to be made when the outcome is important. Let's look at these decisions closely and examine a number of successful ways in which to approach them.

What Is a Judgment Call?

Judgment calls are made all the time. Everyone has to make a judgment call from time to time. As a law enforcement officer, you will be called on to make numerous judgment calls on issues ranging from whether to arrest someone to how to resolve a dispute. But the judgment calls that law enforcement officers are called on to make tend to have a number of things in common. For instance:

- the stakes are high
- the information you need is incomplete or ambiguous

- the people involved disagree about them
- there are often ethical dilemmas and/or conflicting values involved
- time is not on your side

How can you make a judgment call with so much uncertainty surrounding the issue? Remember that these types of decisions, however difficult, are made all the time. Each one has an outcome that is both subjective and debatable. That is, judgment calls are not made purely on facts because the facts are not completely available. They are debatable because another person, who knows as much as you do about the decision and the situation surrounding it, could come up with a strong argument as to why your decision might be wrong (or another option is right). Accepting the nature of judgment calls before you make them can help take some of the stress out of the decision-making process.

Preparing to Make a Judgment Call

In many situations law enforcement officers are called on to resolve, you can't always gather all the pertinent information needed to come to an informed and logical decision. Perhaps the facts are incomplete and the problem needs to be resolved right now. But how can you make a good decision under these circumstances? Is there a way to prepare to make a good judgment call? The answer is yes. You will not end up with all the facts, because they are not always clear, and it is debatable what to include and what to exclude. But arming yourself with information is still an important step toward making such decision. Let's consider a real-life example as we explore the preparation for a judgment call.

Example

A family dispute ensues between a husband and his wife. They have been married for 12 years and have three young children. The children are in the house with their mother when you arrive. The husband is sitting out on the porch. As you begin to interview him about what happened, the wife comes out and starts yelling. The husband responds and the arguing erupts again. You tell the wife to go back inside and you keep them separated. The wife tells you that her husband has been drinking and he is very nasty when he drinks. He yells at her and the kids for no reason and has even kicked the dog in the past. She wants him to go sleep it off somewhere and come back in the morning when he is sober. You approach the husband and get his version of the story. He tells you his version of the facts and says that he just wants to make up with his wife. Satisfied that he is intoxicated and that no crime has been committed, you ask him if he can stay with a friend or relative for the night. He says, "This is my house, I don't want to leave in the middle of the night and wake up my friend. Can I just stay and go to bed?" What are you going to do? If he stays, the fight will likely continue and may even escalate. No crime has been committed, so you can't arrest him and you have no legal authority to make him leave.

This is a great example of a real-life judgment call that law enforcement officers are called on to make every day. The first step, although it will not be as complete as with other types of decisions, is to gather information. Decide what kinds of data you need and try at this point to determine what you will base your decision on. In this step, you want to identify all available options. Let's look at one possible thought process next.

Process

First, you need to decide whether you have a legal obligation to act. No crime has been committed, so an arrest is not called for. Next, you should take into account what each person wants, including yourself. The wife wants him to sober up somewhere else and come back in the morning. He just wants to make up with his wife. You want the fighting to stop in this household for the night.

The second step is to gather more information. Ask the wife if this has ever happened before and if so, what was done. Ask if her husband has friends or relatives in the area. You might discover better or more sources of data, find out about further options, or realize that you did not consider an important aspect of the decision.

The third step is to play "what if?" Explore each option as a solution, asking yourself how this option would work as a solution. Who would benefit? Who would be hurt, annoyed, or wronged? What is the best-case scenario and what is the worst for your option? Test each possibility and weigh its possible benefits and detriments. How do they measure up to the criteria you established in step one?

In this case, the best-case scenario is that he stays at a friend's house for the night and comes home sober. This will ensure that there is no more arguing tonight and it ensures that he will be sober when he returns. Now imagine the worst case. He stays in the house, drinks more, and a fight erupts that now turns physical. Clearly, he must leave for this night.

Practice

You notice a person walking through and looking into numerous back yards in the middle of the night. He is dressed in black and is acting suspiciously. You approach him and he tells you that he is looking for his lost dog. He also knows that he looks suspicious and might be frightening people, so he tells you he is just going to go home for the night and will continue his search in the morning. Do you let him leave? What information would be important to find out in preparing to make the judgment call as to whether you should let him leave or not? Circle as many as apply.

   a. What is his name and where does he live?

   b. Has anyone reported any problems in this neighborhood tonight?

   c. What kind of dog does he own?

   d. Does he have any active wants or warrants?

Answer

Choices **a**, **b**, and **d** would be valuable information to have when preparing to make such as judgment call. Choice **c** is not relevant.

What about Biases and Intuition?

As previously noted, judgment calls are subjective. They are not simply a distillation of the facts. At some point in the decision-making process, you will probably make choices that are not easy. Even after you have obtained your information, and explored the what-if scenarios, the outcome is still your opinion.

In order to make good judgment calls, you need to acknowledge and check your natural inclinations toward decisions. For example, everyone has biases that influence opinion. You might have experienced, for example, the loss of a pet and you might feel pity for this person. Or, you may have been the victim of a burglary that happened just like this scenario. These experiences could cloud your ability to make an effective judgment call.

The problem is that biases, or any type of preexisting attitude, reduce your ability to objectively evaluate information. If you allow them to play an active part in your decisions you run the risk of making a bad choice. When you are aware of your biases you will not eliminate them, but you can check that they are not getting in the way of a good judgment call. What about intuition or instincts? As you go through the process of making a judgment call, you might get a feeling, a hunch, that one option simply feels right when compared to the others even when logic tells you otherwise. Also called a gut reaction, this feeling can lead to a great decision. Many successful law enforcement officers are characterized as having great intuition. However, intuition can also lead to a disaster. As with biases, acknowledge your intuition but listen to it as one factor in many. It should not outweigh the facts and other input you gathered.

Practice

Which is NOT an example of intuition being used to make a judgment call?

a. You pull a car over and something just doesn't seem right. The driver's story does not match the passenger's, this is a high drug trafficking road, and they both look like they have been doing drugs. You decide to search the car for drugs.

b. You are a prison guard and one of the prisoners is acting strange. He seems to be walking differently and you think he may have a shank hidden in his pants. You decide to search him.

c. You are interviewing a husband about his missing wife. His statements seem contrived and rehearsed. You decide that he is the main suspect in the case.

d. You witness a person selling drugs on a street corner. You pull up to him, search him, and find the drugs.

Answer

Choice **d** is not an example of intuition. Your actions were based on fact because you witnessed him selling drugs.

Making the Call

You can prepare as thoroughly as humanly possible before making a judgment call, getting input and information from dozens of sources, evaluating each option as carefully as possible. But it still comes down to your opinion. How do you make the leap to a decision? Here are a couple more ideas that can help.

Evaluate the Risks

After you have looked at each option in terms of what-if, determining who (or what) will gain or lose from possible outcomes, you should look at your decision in terms of risk: How much risk are you willing to take? Are you willing to suffer the consequences if you make the wrong choice?

In law enforcement, these consequences can range from being disciplined to losing your job. Not to mention that someone can get hurt, including you. For example, you suspect that the person you just pulled over is wanted for kidnapping. The choice is whether to get him out of the car, handcuff him, and hold him there until you can determine whether he is indeed wanted. The best-case scenario is that he is wanted and you catch a serious criminal. The worst-case scenario is that he is the kidnapper and you have just let him go. Notice that the risk occurs if you decide to let him go and he is the kidnapper. Therefore, in this case, you need to decide whether you can tolerate the risk of having the worst-case scenario occur. If you can't, you should not let him go. The best question to ask yourself, "If I take the risk, what are the potential consequences?"

Here is another scenario: You are a border control agent and have a person you suspect of smuggling contraband stopped at the border attempting to enter the country. He tells you that he was visiting family in Mexico and that he is a U.S. citizen. The line at the border is starting to back up and your supervisor tells you to keep the line short. You need to make a call as to what to do with this person. If you let him go, you risk allowing the contraband to enter the country. If you detain him, the line will continue to grow until you can resolve this problem. Which presents the greatest risk, the contraband or a long line? If you want to make a judgment call based on what will be the least risk, you will detain this person and search his car.

Examine the Consequences

Remember that judgment calls are subjective and debatable. They rely on opinion as well as facts and figures. That is not to say that they rely on hunches or prejudices to make decisions. Using either (or both) does not take into account the objective realities of a situation. Let's go back to the example of the family dispute between a husband and wife. Once you have impartially looked at the situation and the facts surrounding it, the judgment call as to whether to allow the husband to stay in the house or force him to leave comes down to a difficult choice. You could probably form a strong argument for either case, but what if you had to make a choice? One way to help make such a decision is to focus on the consequences. Will anyone be helped or harmed by the decision? Weigh the value and term of the benefit or detriment—is it a convenience or inconvenience, or does it result in a long-term effect? As a law enforcement officer, you have a unique obligation to ensure that no further harm is caused to either party. You must ensure everyone's safety. Therefore, your decision must take into account all possible detrimental outcomes.

In Short

Judgment calls can be difficult. In a situation where the stakes are high, and even the experts disagree, you may not want to make a choice that is, at best, subjective and debatable. But there are many circumstances in which you will have to do just that. You will need to consider any facts you can gather, the advice of others, your intuition, and even your values. Take your time with judgment calls, and with practice, you will become more confident in making them.

SKILL BUILDING UNTIL NEXT TIME

- Although they rely on evidence and prior decisions, judges must make judgment calls frequently. Check the newspaper for a complicated case and find out more information about it online. Look at the evidence that was presented by both sides. On what do you think the judge based his or her decision?
- Have you ever downloaded music from the Internet without permission? Maybe you know someone who has. Was the decision a judgment call? If so, how did you come to your decision?

15 ▶ Why Did It Happen?

LESSON SUMMARY

In this lesson, you'll learn how explanations are different from arguments. You'll also learn the criteria for determining whether the explanation you're being offered is good or bad.

As a law enforcement officer, you will often deal with people's explanations about why something happened. For example, an inmate may attempt to tell you why he was involved in a fight with a fellow inmate or a kid may try to tell you why he broke a window. In both cases, you will be called upon to listen to and evaluate an explanation.

Explanations are very closely related to arguments, but they're not quite the same thing. Whereas an argument generally aims to convince you that a certain claim is true, an explanation aims to convince you *why* a claim is true. For example, compare the following two statements:

1. You should be more careful going down these stairs. They're steep and lots of people fall.
2. He fell down the stairs because they're very steep and he wasn't careful.

The first example is an argument. The writer is trying to convince you to be more careful on the stairs (conclusion) because the steps are steep (premise) and lots of people fall (premise). The second example is an explanation. The writer here is telling you *why* someone fell down the stairs—because they're steep and because he wasn't careful.

So, explanations are different from arguments. But what does this have to do with critical thinking and reasoning skills?

Well, just as you will be presented with arguments of all types almost every day of your law enforcement career, you will also be presented with explanations of all kinds. And just as you need to evaluate arguments carefully before you decide whether to accept them, you should also evaluate explanations carefully before you decide whether they're valid.

When it comes to explanations, there are four criteria that you should look for:

1. relevance
2. testability
3. circularity
4. compatibility with existing knowledge

Relevance

One of the first tests any explanation should undergo is the test for **relevance**. Is the explanation that is provided clearly relevant to the issue being explained? That is, is there a clear and obvious connection between the issue and the explanation?

For example, in explaining a fight, an inmate may say to you, "I punched him because he tried to kill me." Is that relevant? Absolutely. People have the right to defend themselves, even prisoners. However, an explanation like the following is certainly *not* relevant:

I punched him because I was late to mess hall.

Being late to lunch does not justify lashing out and punching another inmate. This is obvious, of course, but that doesn't prevent people from offering irrelevant explanations.

Practice

1. Provide another relevant and another irrelevant reason for one inmate punching another.

Relevant: _____

Irrelevant: _____

Answer

1. Answers will vary. You might have written something like the following:
Relevant: He was attempting to steal my radio.
Irrelevant: He is new to the system.

One important thing to keep in mind about explanations is that an explanation can pass the relevancy test and still not be a *good* explanation. For example, "I punched him because he punched my friend" is not a *good* explanation, but it is a *relevant* explanation—because you punched him in retaliation.

Practice

Read the following explanations carefully. Are they relevant (**R**) or irrelevant (**I**)?

_____ **2.** I didn't go because it was snowing heavily outside.

_____ **3.** I didn't get accepted into the academy because I didn't get my application in on time.

_____ **4.** I didn't pass the entrance exam because it was my friend's birthday.

Answers

2. R. Bad weather is a relevant explanation for not going somewhere. Snow can affect the driving conditions and make it dangerous to go anywhere.

3. R. Not getting an application in by a deadline is a relevant explanation for failing to get accepted into a program.

4. I. Failing an entrance exam has nothing to do with your friend's birthday.

Testability

You may not be a scientist, but you've certainly performed some experiments in your life. You may have bought different brands of detergent, for example, to see which brand got your clothes cleaner. Or you may have tried different cold medicines to see which worked best for you. This type of experimenting enables you to explain why you use the brand you use: "I use Rinse-All because it doesn't bother my sensitive skin," for example. This explanation is one that can be tested. It therefore passes the next test of validity for explanations: **testability**.

Testability is as important as relevance when it comes to evaluating explanations. If someone provides an explanation that is impossible to test, you should be highly suspicious. An untestable explanation is one that is impossible to verify through experimentation. And that's precisely why you should be on guard.

For example, recall the infamous Son of Sam homicides. When asked to explain why he killed, David Berkowitz told investigators that his dog told him to do it. Is there any way to test this explanation? It can't be verified, but it also can't be refuted. The explanation is untestable (and absurd, but that's another story). Here's another example:

We met because we were meant to meet.

Is there any way to test this explanation? No. There's no test for fate, after all. Though it may be romantic, this is an untestable—and therefore invalid—explanation.

Practice

Read the following explanations carefully. Are they testable (**T**) or untestable (**U**)?

_____ **5.** You won the competition because it was in the stars.

_____ **6.** I got the job as a police officer because I had all the qualifications they were looking for.

_____ **7.** I passed the exam because I studied.

_____ **8.** You didn't get hurt because luck was on your side.

Answers

5. U. There's no way to verify that something happened because it was in the stars.

6. T. This can be verified. You can ask your employer why he or she chose you for the job.

7. T. This can be verified. You can experiment with studying versus not studying.

8. U. There's no way to verify if luck is ever on anyone's side.

Circularity

In Lesson 12, "Logical Fallacies: The Impostors," you learned about circular reasoning: arguments that double back on themselves because the conclusion and the premise say essentially the same thing. Explanations can be circular, too. The inmate may offer the following explanation for throwing a punch: "I punched him because we were fighting." That's a **circular explanation**. "I punched him" and "we were fighting" say essentially the same thing.

The so-called explanation simply restates the situation—it doesn't explain it, and that doesn't make for a valid explanation. Here's another example:

The inflation was caused by an increase in prices.

Notice that "inflation" and "increase in prices" are essentially the same thing. Once again, this is an explanation that goes in a circle. The explanation does not offer any insight as to how or why the situation occurred.

Practice

Read the explanations below carefully. Identify explanations that pass (**P**) the logic test and those that fail (**F**) because they are circular.

_____ **9.** He has insomnia because he has trouble sleeping.

_____ **10.** She's a genius because she's smart.

_____ **11.** They work well together because they share the same goals.

_____ **12.** He keeps the birds in separate cages because he doesn't want to keep them together.

_____ **13.** He got sick because he didn't dress warmly enough.

Answers

9. F. "Insomnia" and "has trouble sleeping" are two ways of saying the same thing.

10. F. Being a genius and being smart are just about the same, so there's no real explanation given here.

11. P. This explanation gives a reason that explains why they work well together.

12. F. A good explanation would tell why the birds can't be kept together.

13. P. This gives a reason telling why he got sick.

More Practice

Write two circular explanations of your own on a separate sheet of paper. To see if they're really circular, use this test: Does the explanation (usually the part that comes after the word *because*) really express the same idea as the issue you're supposed to be explaining?

Compatibility with Existing Knowledge

You tell the inmate that he will face severe discipline if he does not give you a better explanation than, "I punched him because we were in a fight." You need to know why the fight started.

He gives another explanation, "I punched him because he was going to kill my family." Sounds like a good explanation at first glance, but on further thought you know it is not valid. The two inmates do not know each other, and they do not know each other's family. This explanation goes against what you know to be true.

Scientific discoveries and technological breakthroughs often surprise people and sometimes shatter theories that were long thought to be true. Remember, people once believed that the Earth was flat. Still, in everyday life, it's a good idea to be wary of explanations that go against what you know from your past experience or from your education.

For example, if you know that the office copier was just fixed this morning, and your assistant says she didn't finish the copies you requested because the copier is broken, you have good reason to doubt the validity of her explanation. Similarly, if your neighbor tells you that gravity is actually caused by a giant U-shaped magnet located at the center of the Earth, you should be highly suspicious, since his explanation conflicts with accepted scientific theories about the makeup of the Earth's interior.

Some explanations, however, may sound odd or surprising to you without necessarily contradicting what you know from your experience or education. In this case, it's probably best to suspend your judgment anyway, until you can verify the explanation. Like *tentative truths*, these explanations might be valid, but you need to learn more before accepting them as true. For example, imagine that the inmate now tells you, "I punched him because he was stealing money from me." You know that things like this happen in prison. Depending on the credibility of the inmate, you could:

- accept that explanation as fact
- accept that explanation as a tentative truth
- reject the explanation, especially if that inmate has a history of lying

In a case like this, the credibility of the person offering the explanation is a key factor. It's important to note, though, that this is not an untestable explanation. You could investigate the incident further, talk to other inmates, or watch CCTV video to find out whether the inmate was telling the truth.

Practice

Consider the following explanations and their sources. Are they acceptable? Why or why not?

14. Your long-time coworker and friend says: "I'm sorry I can't cover your shift tomorrow. I have a doctor's appointment and I can't reschedule again."

15. Your local garage mechanic says: "Your car broke down because your transmission is shot. It's going to need a lot of work."

16. Your neighbor says: "I don't exercise because it's bad for your health. It wears your body down."

Answers

14. If you've worked with this person for a long time and consider her a friend, then this explanation is acceptable.

15. The acceptability of this explanation would depend partly on how much you know about cars. A ruined transmission is a very costly repair. If you don't know much about cars and don't know your mechanic very well, it might be good to get a second opinion.

16. Unacceptable. All evidence points to exercise as a key to improving health and living a longer life.

In Short

Explanations, much like arguments, need to meet certain criteria before you should feel comfortable accepting them. To be valid, an explanation should be **relevant**—clearly related to the event or issue in question—and **testable**—able to be verified in some way. **Circular explanations**—ones that double back on themselves like circular arguments—should be rejected, and you should be careful about accepting explanations that contradict your knowledge or accepted theories.

SKILL BUILDING UNTIL NEXT TIME

- Pay attention to the explanations around you: at home, at work, at school, and on television. See how often you find people offering explanations that don't meet the criteria discussed in this lesson.
- Once again, sitcoms can help you sharpen your critical thinking and reasoning skills. Characters on sitcoms often find themselves in situations where they have to come up with a quick explanation—and usually those explanations are quite bad. Be on the lookout for these explanations and use the criteria you've learned to evaluate them. Are they relevant? Circular? Testable? Just plain absurd?

16 ▶ Inductive Reasoning

LESSON SUMMARY

In this lesson, you'll review the difference between deductive and inductive reasoning. You'll also sharpen your inductive reasoning skills by learning how to draw logical conclusions from evidence.

This lesson deals with **inductive arguments**. As we mentioned in Lesson 7, inductive arguments are the key to a law enforcement officer's job. The reason for this is clear—law enforcement officers must not jump to conclusions. Instead, they must allow the evidence to bring them to a logical conclusion.

Reasoning that begins by drawing a conclusion is known as deductive reasoning. In deductive reasoning, as you know, an argument moves from a conclusion to the evidence (premises) that supports that conclusion. You should be familiar with deductive reasoning, as it formed the basis of the last few lessons. If you are still having trouble, make sure you review these lessons.

Inductive arguments move from evidence to a conclusion drawn from that evidence. As a critical thinker, when you come across a deductive argument, you should examine the validity of the *evidence* for the conclusion. If the evidence is valid, the conclusion—and therefore the whole argument—is a good one.

However, in inductive reasoning, the goal is not to test the validity of the evidence. Rather, it is to examine the validity of the *conclusion*. If the conclusion stems logically from the evidence, then the argument can be considered a good one.

But how do you know if the conclusion is logical? In inductive reasoning, the main criterion is to determine the **likelihood** that the premises lead to the conclusion. Likelihood can be judged based on:

- common sense
- past experience

Of course, formal logic, involving mathematical symbols, can also help, but that is not discussed in this book, as it will have no direct effect on your future career and your current success on law enforcement entrance exams. Here's an example of a brief inductive argument:

> Recently, several states have passed laws banning text messaging while driving. A lot of people must have been getting into car accidents as a result of being distracted by text messaging while driving.

If the premise that there was a major power outage in a nearby town is true, is it reasonable to assume that a lot of people were getting into car accidents due to text messaging? What do *you* think—is texting while driving likely to cause a traffic accident? Based on common sense and past experience, you can say *yes* with confidence. Is it very likely? Again, you can confidently say *yes*. Therefore, this is a good inductive argument—a logical conclusion drawn from common sense and past experience, or from substantial evidence.

The Science of Inductive Reasoning

Any time someone draws conclusions from evidence, inductive reasoning is being used. Scientists use it all the time. For example, let's say a scientist takes two equally healthy plants of the same size, age, and type. She puts Plant A in a room with a radio that plays only classical music. She puts Plant B in a room with a radio that plays only rock and roll. Both plants receive equal light and water. After six weeks, Plant A has grown six inches. Plant B, on the other hand, has grown only three inches, which is the average growth rate for these types of plants. She repeats this experiment and gets the same results. Using her inductive reasoning skills, what is the most logical thing for the scientist to conclude?

a. In both cases, Plant B must not have been as healthy as Plant A when the experiment began.
b. Plants grow better when exposed to classical music than to rock and roll.
c. Rock and roll music stunts plant growth.

Well, common sense would suggest that choice **a** isn't an option, because it is stated that both plants were equally healthy at the start of the experiment. Furthermore, since it is known that Plant B grew at the *normal* rate, then **c** can't be a logical conclusion, either. But even without this process of elimination, common sense and the results of the two experiments point to conclusion **b**, that plants grow better to classical music than to rock and roll. (This is true, by the way!)

Of course, this conclusion would be even more valid if the scientist repeated the experiment several more times and continued to get the same results. The more she performs the experiment and gets the same results, the stronger her argument will be.

Elementary, My Dear Watson

Detectives, like scientists, also use inductive reasoning. In the following excerpt from the story "The Reigate Puzzle," for example, the famous fictional character Sherlock Holmes uses inductive reasoning to solve a tricky crime. By examining a piece of a torn document, he is able to conclude that *two* different men wrote the document, and he's able to determine which of the two men is the ringleader. Read how he does it:

"And now I made a very careful examination of the corner of paper which the Inspector had submitted to us. It was at once clear to me that it formed part of a very remarkable document. Here it is. Do you not now observe something very suggestive about it?" [said Holmes.]

"It has a very irregular look," said the Colonel.

"My dear sir," cried Holmes, "there cannot be the least doubt in the world that it has been written by two persons doing alternate words. When I draw your attention to the strong *t*'s of 'at' and 'to,' and ask you to compare them with the weak ones of 'quarter' and 'twelve,' you will instantly recognize the fact. A very brief analysis of these four words would enable you to say with the utmost confidence that the 'learn' and the 'maybe' are written in the stronger hand, and the 'what' in the weaker."

"By Jove, it's as clear as day!" cried the Colonel. "Why on earth should two men write a letter in such a fashion?"

"Obviously the business was a bad one, and one of the men who distrusted the other was determined that, whatever was done, each should have an equal hand in it. Now, of the two men, it is clear that the one who wrote the 'at' and 'to' was the ringleader."

"How do you get at that?"

"We might deduce it from the mere character of the one hand as compared with the other. But we have more assured reasons than that for supposing it. If you examine this scrap with attention you will come to the conclusion that the man with the stronger hand wrote all of his words first, leaving blanks for the other to fill up. These blanks were not always sufficient, and you can see that the second man had to squeeze to fit his 'quarter' in between the 'at'

and the 'to,' showing that the latter were already written. The man who wrote all his words first is undoubtedly the man who planned the affair."

Notice how Holmes looks carefully at the document and uses what he sees to make logical inferences (draw logical conclusions) about the two men responsible for the crime. The difference in the *t*'s indicates two different writers and the uneven spacing of the words indicates who wrote first, thus leading Holmes to conclude that the man who wrote first was the man "who planned the affair."

Practice

Now it is your turn to play detective and use your reasoning skills to draw logical inferences. Read carefully the information you are given (the premises) and consider what would be the most logical conclusion to draw from that evidence.

1. Every time it rains outside, your bad knee starts to ache. When you wake up this morning, you find that your bad knee is sore. You can therefore logically conclude that
   a. today is going to be a clear, sunny day.
   b. it's going to rain today.
   c. there is a lot of humidity in the air.

2. Every Thursday, a man waits outside a check cashing store and robs female patrons as they walk out after cashing their checks. You are a detective assigned to the case and it is Thursday. You go by the check cashing store and see a man and woman involved in a struggle. What can you logically conclude?
   a. They are a husband and wife involved in a domestic argument.
   b. He is robbing her.
   c. They are involved in a disagreement.

3. The last two times the members of two certain gangs were allowed out in the yard together, they got into a fight. Members of the two gangs have just been let out in the yard today. You can therefore logically conclude that
   a. you should be on the lookout for a fight.
   b. you shouldn't worry, today may be different.
   c. you should warn them against fighting.

4. If the fight was caused because the two gangs were wearing colors the last few times and today they are all in the same prison uniform, would you still worry? Why or why not?

5. You are a K-9 officer and Max is your drug-sniffing dog. Every time Max senses drugs, he barks and sits down. Today, you and Max are at the local mall. You walk past a man with a large briefcase. Max starts to bark at the briefcase and sits down. You can therefore logically conclude that
   a. the man has dog bones in the briefcase.
   b. the briefcase is actually a cat carrier and Max is barking at the cat.
   c. the man has drugs in the briefcase.

Answers

1. It would be most logical to conclude choice **b**, that it is going to rain today. Choice **c** is another possibility, but because it always rains when your knee hurts, **b** is a more likely possibility.

2. The most logical choice is **b**, he is robbing her. Although choices **a** and **b** are always possibilities, you know that a robbery pattern exists in this situation, making **b** the best choice.

3. Based on your last two experiences, the best choice is **a**. Choice **b** is irresponsible and choice **c** is okay, but may not stop a fight.

4. If it can be shown that they were fighting with each other just because of their colors, then a uniform would solve the problem. Therefore, you may not have to worry as much today because they are not in their colors.

5. The most logical thing to conclude would be choice **c**. Choice **b** is likely but not probable, especially because your dog is trained to ignore other animals. Choice **a** is unlikely. Although a possibility, it would not be the most logical conclusion to draw.

In Short

Inductive reasoning is the process of drawing conclusions from evidence. A good inductive argument is one in which it is very likely that the premises lead to the conclusion. Past experience and common sense can be used to measure that likelihood.

SKILL BUILDING UNTIL NEXT TIME

- Notice how often you use inductive reasoning throughout your day. At home, work, or school, as you travel from place to place, what conclusions do you draw from what you see around you?
- Read a detective story or watch a detective show like *Cold Case*, or *Law & Order*. Pay special attention to how detectives use evidence to draw conclusions about the crimes.

17 ▶ Jumping to Conclusions

LESSON SUMMARY

Just as there are logical fallacies to beware of in deductive reasoning, there are several logical fallacies to look out for in inductive reasoning. This lesson shows you how to recognize and avoid those fallacies.

Imagine that you are a border control agent working in Arizona. You and a newly transferred agent are talking. He says, "At my last post, we had a few agents get seriously injured during an incident when they tried to stop some illegal immigrants from crossing the border. You have got to watch your back; all these immigrants are criminals and will hop on any chance you give them." Do you really believe that all immigrants are criminals? Does he? More than likely not, but he has just been caught jumping to conclusions.

Inductive reasoning, as you know, is all about drawing conclusions from evidence. But sometimes, people draw conclusions that aren't quite logical. That is, conclusions are drawn too quickly or are based on the wrong kind of evidence. This lesson introduces you to the three logical fallacies that lead to illogical conclusions in inductive reasoning: *hasty generalizations*, *biased generalizations*, and *non sequiturs*.

Hasty Generalizations

A **hasty generalization** is a conclusion that is based on too little evidence. Your coworker's conclusion about the criminality of immigrants is a hasty generalization. He'd only seen one incident occur involving immigrants in his entire time working as an agent. Has he fairly characterized everyone that crossed the border? No. First of all, he's only witnessed one incident during his entire career. Second, he needs to also think about all the other thousands of interactions he and others have had that have not ended in violence. Only after he has taken into account all this other evidence will he have enough premises to lead to a logical conclusion.

Here's another example of a hasty generalization. Let's say you're introduced to a woman named Ellen at work, and she barely acknowledges you. You decide she's cold and arrogant. Is your conclusion fair? Maybe Ellen was preoccupied. Maybe she was sick. Maybe she had a big meeting she was heading to. Who knows? The point is, you only met her once, and you drew a conclusion about her based on too little evidence.

A few weeks later, you meet Ellen again. This time, she's friendly. She remembers meeting you, and you have a pleasant conversation. Suddenly you have to revise your conclusion about her, don't you? Now you think she's nice. But the next time you see her, she doesn't even say hello. What's happening here? You keep jumping to conclusions about Ellen. But you really need to have a sufficient number of encounters with her before you can come to any conclusions.

Hasty generalizations have a lot in common with stereotypes. In the case of stereotypes, conclusions about an entire group are drawn based on a small segment of that group. Likewise, hasty generalizations draw conclusions about something based on too small a sample—one incident at the border, or two or three encounters with Ellen.

Here are a few more hasty generalizations:

Brandon is a jock, and he's a lousy student. All jocks are lousy students.

Suzie is blonde, and she always seems to have so much fun. So I guess it's true that blondes have more fun.

You'd need to see a lot more examples of jocks and blondes before either of these conclusions could be justified.

Practice

Are any of the following hasty generalizations?

1. I saw that video of what the police did to Rodney King. All cops are racist.

2. That guy is wearing red. That's the color of the Blood gang. He must be a Blood.

3. Jack has been arrested for selling drugs over 30 times. I just saw him hand someone a package. It must have been drugs.

Answers

1. Yes, this is a hasty generalization. Not all cops are racist.
2. This is a hasty generalization as well. Not all people who wear red are Bloods.
3. This is not a hasty generalization. Jack is a known drug dealer with a long rap sheet. He is more than likely selling drugs again.

Biased Generalizations

You read a headline that says, "85% of Americans believe that prison is too harsh." As a corrections officer, this intrigues you. As you read on, you notice that the survey only interviewed prisoners. Should you be swayed by these findings? Obviously not. Of course, prisoners are going to say that life in prison is too harsh.

The problem with a survey like this (there will be more on surveys in Lesson 19, "Numbers Never Lie") is that the pool of people it surveyed was *biased*. Think about it for a moment. Prisoners are going to say prison is too harsh because they hope it will potentially lead to more lax conditions for them. Therefore, the conclusion that the majority of Americans believe that prison is too harsh is biased as well. It's based on a survey of biased respondents and, as a result, cannot be considered representative of Americans as a whole.

Biased generalizations can be made without using surveys as well. Any conclusion based on the testimony of someone who is biased is a **biased generalization**. For example, imagine you are a police officer and you tell your friend at work that you are transferring to the Internal Investigations Division.

"Internal Investigations—are you kidding me?!" he responds. "I've had run-ins with them; they are just a bunch of rats and tattletales."

Should your friend's reaction change your mind about transferring? Probably not. Your reasoning skills should tell you that your friend's conclusion about Internal Investigations might be biased. If he had a good experience with the squad, he would probably have a better opinion about it.

Let's look at another example. Read the following inductive argument carefully:

All my friends say studying for law enforcement entrance exams is a waste of time. So I guess

you shouldn't bother studying if you don't want to waste your time.

How could this be a biased generalization? Write your answer below.

_____
_____
_____
_____
_____

If this conclusion is based on evidence from biased sources, then the generalization (the conclusion) is biased. For example, if those friends who say that studying is a waste of time are also friends who have studied but failed the exam, then they're likely to have a negative (biased) opinion of studying. Hence, their conclusion would be biased.

But how could this be a *reliable* inductive argument? Write your answer below.

_____
_____
_____
_____
_____

If all the friends had passed entrance exams, then this would be a much more reliable conclusion. If all the friends had passed several different exams, it would be even more reliable; their conclusion would represent a broader range of experience.

To avoid being biased, then, conclusions should be drawn only from a sample that's truly representative of the subject at hand.

Practice

Are any of the following biased generalizations?

4. A police officer to a coworker: "Any car on the road at 4 A.M. is being driven by a drunk driver."

5. An employee who was laid off from his job: "That company is a terrible place to work. They laid me off!"

6. A criminal defendant to his attorney: "This judge is tough, but fair. Other prisoners have told me that he doesn't mess around, but that in the end he treats you right."

Answers

4. Yes, this is a generalization that is probably biased because the officer has made many DUI arrests at 4 A.M.

5. Yes, this employee's generalization is probably biased. He is making a conclusion based on only one small piece of evidence—his own misfortune at having been laid off. He clearly has negative feelings for the company that may not be justified.

6. This is not biased because it is taking into account other people's experience with the judge.

Non Sequitur

A **non sequitur** is a conclusion that does not follow logically from its premises. The problem with this fallacy is that too much of a jump is made between the premises and the conclusion. Here's an example:

> Johnson is a good family man. Therefore, he will be a good law enforcement officer.

It's great that Johnson is a good family man, but his devotion to his family does not necessarily mean that he'll be a good police officer or corrections officer. Notice that this argument *assumes* that the qualities that make a good family man also make a good law enforcement officer and that's not necessarily, or even probably, the case. Many good family men are lousy law enforcement officers, and many good law enforcement officers are not particularly devoted to their families. The argument makes a leap—a big one—that defies logic. It's certainly possible that Johnson will be a good police officer or corrections officer, but solely judging from the premises, it's not *likely*.

Here's another example of a *non sequitur*:

> Mike is an expert target shooter, so he'd be a great police officer.

This *non sequitur* assumes that people who shoot well make better police officers than those that do not. This may sometimes be true, but it is not always the case. Furthermore, even if he is an expert target shooter, being a good police officer requires excellent communication skills, superior problem-solving skills, and dedication, and we have no evidence that Mike has those qualities. Therefore, we can't logically conclude that Mike will be a good police officer.

Here's one more:

> You like cats. Cathy is a cat person, too, so you'll get along well.

What's wrong with this argument? Here, the arguer assumes that because you and Cathy are both cat people, you will get along. But just because you both like cats doesn't mean you'll like each other. It's another *non sequitur*.

Some *non sequiturs* follow the pattern of reversing the premise and conclusion. Read the following argument, for example:

People who succeed always have clear goals. Sandra has clear goals, so she'll succeed.

Here's the argument broken down:

Premise 1: People who succeed always have clear goals.
Premise 2: Sandra has clear goals.
Conclusion: Sandra will succeed.

Although at first glance the example may seem reasonable, in actuality, it doesn't make logical sense. That's because premise 2 and the conclusion *reverse* the claim set forth in premise 1. When parts of a claim are reversed, the argument does not stay the same. It's like saying that geniuses often have trouble in school, so someone who is having trouble in school is a genius, and that's just not logical.

In Sandra's case, your critical thinking and reasoning skills should also tell you that simply because she set clear goals for herself doesn't mean they'll be achieved; hard work and dedication are also factors in the formula for success. Furthermore, the definition of *success* is something everyone determines for him- or herself.

Practice

Are there any *non sequiturs* in the following arguments?

7. Paula can run a 7-minute mile. She'll make a great corrections officer.

8. That car is a stick shift. Most stick shift cars get better gas mileage than automatics. You'll probably get better gas mileage if you get a stick shift.

9. Most state troopers that I have seen are over 6′2″ tall. You're 6′5″, so you would make a great state trooper.

Answers

7. Yes, this is a *non sequitur*.
8. No, this is not a *non sequitur*.
9. Yes, this is a *non sequitur*.

Practice

What assumptions do the *non sequiturs* in items 7 and 9 make?

Answers

Argument number 7 assumes that people who are excellent runners will also make excellent corrections officers. But being a corrections officer requires more than running fast. It also involves communication skills, an ability to handle crises, skill in dealing with people, and much more.

In argument number 9, the second premise and conclusion reverse the first premise. Just because you are tall doesn't mean that you would make a great state trooper.

In Short

When it comes to inductive arguments, you need to be on the lookout for three kinds of logical fallacies. **Hasty generalizations** draw conclusions from too little evidence. **Biased generalizations** draw conclusions from *biased* evidence. Finally, ***non sequiturs*** jump to conclusions that defy logic; they make assumptions that don't hold water.

SKILL BUILDING UNTIL NEXT TIME

- The next time you meet someone for the first time, be aware of how you form an opinion of him or her. Do you jump to conclusions, or do you wait until you've gathered more evidence to decide whether he or she would make a good friend or colleague?
- Teach a friend what you learned in this lesson. Give your friend a few of your own examples of the three fallacies.

18 ▶ More Inductive Reasoning

LESSON SUMMARY

This lesson discusses the inductive reasoning approach to determining causes. It also goes over some of the common mistakes in reasoning people make when determining cause and effect.

I n Lesson 15, "Why Did It Happen?" you learned about how explanations are different from arguments. This lesson looks at a specific type of argument: the **causal argument**. The main difference between an explanation and a causal argument is simply in the way the argument is arranged. In an explanation, like in deductive reasoning, you look at the conclusion ("I punched him") and then test the validity of the premises ("because he was going to kill me"). In a causal argument, on the other hand, the inductive approach is used: Evidence (what happened) is looked at, a conclusion is drawn about the cause based on that evidence, and then the validity of that conclusion is considered.

Just as there are criteria for testing explanations, there are also strategies for evaluating causes. Similarly, just as explanations can use false reasoning, there are also logical fallacies that can be committed in causal arguments. This chapter starts by addressing the two main strategies for determining cause and then discusses how to avoid the fallacies that often go with them.

Determining Cause

When you are presented with an effect and want to inductively determine the cause, there are generally two techniques to use: looking for what's different and looking for what's the same.

Looking for the Difference

Your car wasn't running well on Wednesday. Normally, you use Ultra-Plus gasoline from the station down the street, but on Tuesday, you were low on gas and on cash, so you pulled into a station near your office and got half a tank of the cheapest gas. On Thursday, you went back to your regular station and filled up with your normal gas. By Friday, the car was running fine again. You did nothing else to your car, and nothing else was out of the ordinary. So what caused the problem?

If you guessed it was the cheap gasoline, you're probably right. Although there are many things that can go wrong with a car and only a thorough inspection could tell for sure, the given evidence points to the cheap gas as the culprit. Why? Because the cheap gas is the **key difference**. Let's recap the facts: Your car ran well on your usual gas. When you changed the brand and grade, your car didn't run well. When you went back to your usual gas, your car ran fine again. The only difference is the gasoline. Therefore, it's logical to conclude that the gasoline caused your car to run less smoothly.

Although in this example it's obvious that the gasoline was the key difference, it isn't always so easy to determine causes. Read the following argument:

> You are a narcotics enforcement officer and you have made over 300 arrests for possession of cocaine during your career. Each time you make an arrest for possession of 3 grams or less, you go before Judge Smith. He listens to your testimony and that of the defendant. Since you always have solid cases with undeniable evidence, he finds in your favor and sentences the defendant to 1 to 3 years in prison. Today, Judge Smith is sick and is not holding court. You have a trial for possession of 2 ounces of cocaine and it is scheduled to be heard by Judge Jones. He listens to your testimony and that of the defendant and he finds in your favor. He sentences the defendant to 5 years of probation. You are very angry and conclude that, "Judge Jones is soft on crime."

This does seem like a logical conclusion based on the evidence and your past experience. After all, what's different between today's case and all the other cases that you brought before the court? The only difference was the judge, so that was the cause. Right? Not necessarily. It is quite possible that had your case been heard by Judge Smith, the defendant would be in prison. However, this conclusion can't be accepted without reservation—you can't say it's *likely* that Judge Jones is to blame. That is, until you ask a key question:

> Were there any other relevant differences that may have caused the lighter sentence?

In other words, you need to consider whether there could have been something else that led to the more lenient sentence. For example, maybe the defendant had a superior defense attorney or maybe he had been successfully treated for his addiction problem prior to the trial.

The more possibilities there are, the less confident you should be that Judge Jones is to blame. However, if there isn't anything else unusual that you can think of, and especially if the next defendant you bring before this judge gets the same sentence, then it's much more likely that the judge is to blame. Either way, before you pinpoint your cause, be sure to consider whether there could be other relevant differences.

Practice

Answer the following questions carefully.

1. Is the following a logical causal argument? Why or why not?

Golden State Prison was the worst prison in the country in terms of violence. In one year alone, the prison experienced 27 assaults, 3 homicides, and 4 guard injuries. Two years ago, a new camera system was installed. Since then, the prison has not experienced any violent incidents. Obviously, the camera system stopped the problems at the prison.

Answer

1. Yes, this is a logical causal argument. Whether it is because prisoners are less likely to resort to violence because now they know they are being watched or guards can more readily identify problems and respond before they escalate into violence, the result is that violence is down. This is a logical conclusion. You should still consider whether there have been other relevant changes in the prison, like new policies, new administration, or new practices.

Looking for the Common Denominator

Sometimes, the cause can be determined not by looking for what's different, but by looking for what's the *same*—that is, something that each incident has in common. Take the following scenario, for example.

There has been a rash of bank robberies occurring in the southeast section of town. The robber, a tall male armed with a silver gun,

gives the teller a note that reads, "Give me your money and no one will get hurt." Tonight, you get a call reporting a bank robbery in the northeast section of town. When you arrive on the scene, the teller hands you the note that the robber gave her. The note has the same wording as those in the southeast robberies and the teller describes the robber as a tall male armed with a silver gun. You conclude that the southeast bank robber has spread out and has now started to rob banks in the northeast section of town.

The note and the description are the **common denominator** for all these occasions. In law enforcement, this is often referred to as a *modus operandi* or *M.O.* It is the criminal's method of operation. Just as it is important to be careful not to overlook other possible differences, however, it's important to remember to look for other possible common denominators. Before you can conclude that the bank robberies are being committed by the same person, you should carefully consider whether there might be anything else in common between the bank robberies.

Practice

Read the following scenario and then answer the questions that follow.

Officer Jones tells you that he hates working on nights when there is a full moon. He says, "For some reason it brings out the worst in people. It's always busy when there is a full moon."

2. Can Officer Jones say with confidence that the full moon is responsible for making the night busy?

3. What other possible common denominators could there be for this apparent relationship?

Answers

2. Officer Jones cannot say this with confidence. First, this explanation is not testable. Second, there are too many other possible explanations.

3. Officer Jones's observation could be caused by other common denominators. Perhaps it is because on nights when there is a full moon, it is brighter outside so more people go out. Or perhaps the full moon happened to fall more often on weekend nights this year.

Post Hoc, Ergo Propter Hoc

Trooper Jones has always been a good worker. He has worked patrol for the past seven years and has never received a complaint. He has consistently received high marks on his performance evaluations and has been cited for meritorious conduct several times. He has multiple goals, but foremost among these is becoming a homicide investigator. One day, Trooper Jones is called on to provide security for the governor. He attends several occasions with him and returns to patrol in a week. The following week, he is promoted to homicide investigator. Upon hearing this, Trooper Smith says, "He got the promotion because he was the governor's lackey for the past week. It pays to suck up."

Trooper Smith has committed the **post hoc, ergo propter hoc** inductive reasoning fallacy. *Post hoc, ergo propter hoc* literally means *after this, therefore because of this*. Trooper Smith has assumed that because Trooper Jones's promotion came *after* he worked the governor's security detail, his promotion was *caused* by his relationship with the governor. In all likelihood, there were several other causes for his promotion. Primary among these is his past performance. Trooper Jones's record clearly demonstrates that he was a superior employee. Of course, cause and effect is a chronological structure—the cause must come before the effect—but remember that you need to consider other possible causes. Just

because *A* comes before *B* doesn't mean there's a logical connection between the two events. Here's another example of *post hoc*:

> After the Citizens First bill was passed, crime in this area skyrocketed. Funny how the bill that was supposed to *reduce* crime actually *increased* it!

Notice how this argument assumes that because the Citizens First bill came first and the rise in crime came second, one *caused* the other. Proving that there's a link between the two events would not be easy, though, especially since an increased crime rate could be caused by many different factors. In fact, a figure as complicated as crime rate is probably caused by a *multitude* of factors.

What else can you think of that might have caused the increase in crime?

Other possible causes:

_____

_____

_____

_____

You may have listed other possible causes like the following:

- an increase in unemployment
- a recession
- a change in population in the area
- a reduction in the police force

In fact, because human society is so complex, most social issues have multiple causes. In all likelihood, the increase in crime was caused by a combination of these, and possibly other, factors. But the Citizens First bill, unless it specifically cut jobs and reduced the police force, is not to blame. It may have come first, but it's not necessarily the cause.

Practice

Do any of the following causal arguments commit the *post hoc* fallacy?

4. Since the prison added more guards, there have been less fights on the tiers. Looks like that was a good investment.

5. After we got our new vacuum cleaner, our electric bills skyrocketed. That thing might as well suck the money right out of our pockets!

6. Mandy started feeding her two-year-old an extra-fortified oatmeal for breakfast, and as a result, he's grown two inches in the last two months!

Answers

4. This seems like a reasonable argument, not a *post hoc* error. Part of what makes this logical is the fact that adding more guards gives the prisoners less opportunity to fight.

5. *Post hoc.* Chances are that unless you vacuum every room every day and you have a big house, the vacuum cleaner won't have much effect on your electric bill. More likely, your utility company has raised your rates and/or you're simply using your other appliances more.

6. *Post hoc.* Babies grow in fits and starts. Maybe the oatmeal is helping, but there are too many other possible causes for this person to assume the growth is due to the fortified cereal.

The Chicken or the Egg?

A fellow officer looks at you while you are guarding a crime scene and says, "You want to know why there are so many murders? It's because we live in a violent society." Is he correct? Maybe, but then again, this might not necessarily the case.

Before you accept your friend's theory, consider that he could have just as easily argued the reverse:

> "We are living in a violent society because there are so many murders."

Which argument is the right one? Does living in a violent society cause a large number of murders, or do we live in a violent society because there are a large number of murders?

Again, both arguments try to simplify a topic that's very complicated. It's very hard to know what came first, a violent society or a large number of murders—the **chicken or egg dilemma**. You need to think carefully about the relationship between the two events before you come to any conclusions.

Here's another example:

> Teenagers are angrier these days because they watch more violent television programs.

Sounds logical, doesn't it? Being exposed to more images of violence can lead to anger issues. But it is also true that someone who is angry might be attracted to violent television programs and therefore, watch more of them. So this is another case where cause and effect could go either way. In such a case, it's best to suspend judgment about the cause until more information is known.

Practice

Read the following carefully. Are any guilty of taking sides in the chicken or egg dilemma?

7. People don't have family values anymore. That's because so many people get divorced these days.

8. Since Linda started exercising, she feels a lot better about herself.

9. There are so many gun manufacturers because the cost of producing guns is so low.

Answers

7. Guilty. It's just as easy to argue that so many people get divorced these days because people don't have family values anymore. As with any social issue, there are certain to be multiple causes.

8. Although it *is* possible to argue the reverse, it's pretty likely that Linda's exercise is indeed responsible for her increased self-esteem.

9. Guilty. This is another chicken or egg dilemma. The low cost of producing guns could just as likely be the result of so many different companies working to develop more cost-effective products and procedures. This case needs further investigation.

In Short

There are two main approaches to determining causes in inductive reasoning: looking for what's different and looking for the common denominator. It is important to remember to look for other possible differences or common causes. Causal arguments should avoid the *post hoc, ergo propter hoc* fallacy, which assumes that because A came before B, A caused B. Finally, some causal arguments fall into the **chicken or egg** trap, where the argument that A caused B is just as strong as the argument that B caused A. Think carefully before accepting such an argument.

SKILL BUILDING UNTIL NEXT TIME

- Be on the lookout this week for errors in causal reasoning. People are often quick to assign cause and neglect to think about other possible differences or common denominators. See if you can catch others—or even yourself—making these mistakes, and correct them.
- Read some history. Historical texts explore cause and effect in detail, and they'll help you see just how complicated causes can sometimes be. This will help you realize how careful you need to be when evaluating cause and effect.

19 ▶ Numbers Never Lie

LESSON SUMMARY

Statistics are often used to strengthen arguments—but they aren't always trustworthy. This lesson shows you how to judge the validity of statistics and how to make sure that any statistics you cite are credible.

There is strength in numbers. This is true whether you are walking the beat or watching the yard. Law enforcement officers have always worked together as a team. The more people you have fighting for a cause, the more likely you are to win. There's strength in numbers in arguments, too—statistics generally carry more weight and sound more valid than opinions. That's because numbers look concrete, factual, and objective.

However, numbers are not always to be trusted. Like words, numbers can be—and often are—manipulated. As a critical thinker, you need to be aware of the kinds of tricks numbers can play. As a potential law enforcement officer candidate, you will need to know how to evaluate surveys, statistics, and other figures, as they will often be utilized in questions on your entrance exams.

First Things First: Consider the Source

One of your first priorities when you come across a figure or statistic is to consider the source. Where is this information coming from? You need to know the source so you can consider its credibility.

Figures are often cited without naming their source. This should automatically raise a red flag. When there's no source acknowledged, that figure could come from anywhere. Here's an example:

Eighty percent of all Americans believe that there is too much violence on television.

Our immediate reaction might be to say "Wow! 80%! That's an impressive statistic." But because this claim does not indicate a source, you have to fight your instinct to accept the number as true. The question "Who conducted this survey?" must be answered in order for you to be able to assess the validity of the figure. A figure that isn't backed by a credible source isn't worth much and can't be accepted with confidence. Unfortunately, you have to consider that the claimant could have made it up to give the *appearance* of statistical support for his argument.

If the claimant does provide a source, then the next step is to consider the credibility of that source. Remember, to determine credibility, look for evidence of bias and level of expertise. Here's that statistic again, attributed to two different sources:

1. According to Parents Against Television Violence, 80% of Americans believe that there is too much violence on television.
2. According to a recent University of Minnesota survey, 80% of Americans believe there is too much violence on television.

Would you accept the statistic as offered by source number 1? How about by source number 2?

While both sources may have a respectable level of expertise, it should be acknowledged that the people who conducted the university study probably have a higher level of expertise. More importantly, the source in number 1—Parents Against Television Violence—should encourage you to consider their statistics with caution. Is a group such as PATV likely to be biased on the issue of television violence? Absolutely. Is it possible, then, that such an organization could offer false or misleading statistics to support its cause? Yes. Would it be wise, therefore, to accept this statistic only with some reservations? Yes.

The university's study, however, is much more likely to have been conducted professionally and accurately. Scholarly research is subject to rigorous scrutiny by the academic community, so the university's findings are probably quite accurate and acceptable. There's less reason to suspect bias or sloppy statistical methods.

Practice

Evaluate the following statistics. Are the sources credible? Why or why not?

1. A survey conducted by Ex-Cons Against Capital Punishment shows that 97% of Americans are against capital punishment.

2. According to the Food and Drug Administration, 67% of Americans have smoked marijuana.

Answers

1. This source may have a respectable level of expertise, but you should consider its potential for bias. Given the source, there is a possibility that the survey was skewed to show such a high disapproval rating.
2. Because the FDA is a government organization whose credibility rests on its awareness of food and drug dangers to American citizens, this statistic can probably be trusted.

The Importance of Sample Size

In the ideal survey or opinion poll, *everyone* in the population in question would be surveyed. But since this is often impossible, researchers have to make do by interviewing a **sample** of the population. Unfortunately, this means that their results do not always reflect the sentiment of the entire population.

Obviously, the more people they ask, the more reflective the survey will be of the entire population. For example, let's say you want to know how parents of children in juvenile detention in the state of Pennsylvania feel about removing juvenile boot camps. If 20,000 parents fall into this category, how many should you survey? Two? Two hundred? Two thousand? Twenty thousand? Indeed, how many people you survey depends on the time and money you have to invest in the survey. But under no circumstances would surveying two or two hundred people be sufficient—these numbers represent far too small a percentage of the population that you're surveying. Two thousand is a much better sample, as it constitutes 10% of the population you are trying to reach.

On NBC TV's newsmagazine *Dateline*, commentator Storm Phillips often ends the show with the results of a *Dateline* opinion poll. Before announcing the results, however, *Dateline* tells its viewers exactly how many people were surveyed. That is, *Dateline* lets you know the exact sample size. This practice helps make the reported results more credible and enables you to judge for yourself whether a sample is large enough to be representative of the sentiments of the entire country.

You're probably wondering how much is enough when it comes to sample size. There's no hard and fast rule here except one: The larger your sample size, the better. The bigger the sample, the more likely it is that your survey results will accurately reflect the opinions of the population in question.

Practice

3. Read the following situation carefully and answer the question that follows. You're conducting a survey of local business owners to see how your police department can better serve their needs. There are approximately 5,000 individual business owners in your city. After how many responses would you feel you have a sample large enough to reflect the opinion of the entire business owners' community?
   a. 5
   b. 50
   c. 500
   d. 1,000

Answer

Five hundred responses (**c**) would probably be sufficient to give you a good idea of the overall sentiment in the business community. If you could get 1,000 responses, however, your results would be much more accurate. Both 5 and 50 are far too small for sample sizes in this survey. For example, suppose you decided to interview only 5 business owners and you selected the only 5 business owners in the entire city that think that the police should not carry guns. Should you act upon this finding? Clearly, the answer is no.

Representative, Random, and Biased Samples

Let's say you want to conduct the business community survey but don't have any money to do it. Since you patrol the downtown business district, you decide to simply poll the businesses on your post. Will your results accurately reflect the sentiment of the entire business community in your city?

Regardless of how the business owners on your post feel about this issue, it would be nearly impossible for your survey results to accurately reflect the sentiments of all the business owners in the entire city. Why? Because your sample is not **representative** of the population whose opinion you wish to reflect. In order for your sample to be representative, it should include *all* the various groups and subgroups within the business population. That is, the people in your sample group should represent the people in the whole group. That means, for one thing, that you need to survey business owners from other areas of the city, not just from where you work. There should be business owners from the downtown area, the uptown area, and the outlying areas of the city. In this way, your survey results are more likely to be proportionate to the results you'd get if you were able to survey all business owners.

But how do you get a representative sample for larger populations such as two million parents or, say, one billion in China? Because the range of respondents is so wide, your best bet is to get a **random** sample. By randomly selecting participants, you have the best chance of getting a representative sample because each person in the population has the same chance of being surveyed. Representative and random samples help prevent you from having a **biased** sample. Imagine you read the following:

In a survey of 6,000 city residents, 79% of the respondents say that the Republican mayor has done an outstanding job.

This claim tells us the sample size—6,000, which is a substantive number. But it doesn't tell how the 6,000 residents were chosen to answer the survey. Because the political affiliation and socioeconomic standing of the respondents could greatly influence the results of the survey, it is important to know whether those 6,000 people are varied enough to accurately reflect the sentiment of an entire city.

For example, if all of those 6,000 surveyed were Republicans, of course the percentage of favorable votes would be high; but that doesn't tell much about how people from other political parties feel. Survey another 6,000 residents who are Democrats and you'd come up with a much, much lower number. Why? Because members of this sample group, due to their socioeconomic status and/or their political beliefs, might be biased against a Republican mayor. Thus, it's critical that the sample be as representative as possible, including both Democrats and Republicans, the wealthy and the poor.

How do you know, though, that a survey has used a representative sample? Surveys that have been conducted legitimately will generally be careful to provide you with information about the sample size and population so that their results are more credible to you. You might see something like the following, for example:

- In a recent survey, 500 random shoppers were asked whether they felt the food court in the mall provides a sufficient selection.
- A survey of 3,000 men between the ages of 18 and 21 found that 72% think either that the drinking age should be lowered to 18 or that the draft age should be raised to 21.

Notice how these claims let you know exactly who was surveyed (random shoppers and men between the ages of 18 and 21). Sometimes, they will go even further. This is achieved by mathematically calculating the rate of error. If you have watched election forecasts, you have seen this before. For example, you might see something like the following:

The Democratic candidate for president is projected to have won the state of Massachusetts by a margin of 22%, give or take 5% (they may even write it out: +/– 5%).

This means that they believe that the Democratic candidate for president has won the state by 22% of the vote, but they are 100% certain that the actual margin falls somewhere between 17% and 27%.

SPECIAL NOTE

Beware of call-in surveys and polls that are conducted by mail or that otherwise depend on the *respondents* to take action. Results of these surveys tend to be misleading because those who take the time to return mail-in surveys or make the effort to call, fax, or e-mail a response are often people who feel very strongly about the issue. To assume that the opinions of those people who feel strongly about the issue represents how the entire population feels is risky because it's not very likely that most people in the population feel that way.

Practice

Evaluate the following claims. Do the surveys seem to have representative samples, or could the samples be biased?

4. **Topic:** Should campus security be tighter?
   Population: Female students
   Sample: Women who have been victims of crimes on campus

5. **Topic:** Is parking enforcement in the city too harsh?
   Population: City residents and visitors
   Sample: People randomly stopped on the street in various districts within the city

6. **Topic:** Should the state prison allow longer visits?
   Population: State residents
   Sample: Relatives of prisoners incarcerated at the prison

Answers

4. The sample in this survey is clearly biased. If only women who have been victims of crime on campus are surveyed, the results will certainly reflect dissatisfaction with campus security. Furthermore, unless this is an all-female college, the sample is not representative.

5. The sample in this survey is representative. People randomly stopped on the street in various parts of the city should result in a good mix of residents and visitors with all kinds of backgrounds and parking needs.

6. This sample is not representative. Certainly the relatives of prisoners will want longer visiting hours. This sample is clearly biased.

Comparing Apples and Oranges

In 1950, the cost of housing one prisoner in a secure prison cost $2,000 per year. Today, it costs about $20,000. That's an increase of over 1,000%!

This increase sounds extreme, doesn't it? But is it really as severe as the math makes it seem? Not quite. The problem with this claim is that while the actual price of housing a prisoner for a year may have increased 1,000%, it's not a fair comparison. That's because $2,000 in 1950 had more market value than $2,000 today. In this situation, the actual costs can't legitimately be compared. Instead, the costs have to be compared after they've been *adjusted for inflation*. Because there has been such a long time span and the value of the dollar has declined in the last 30 years, maybe $20,000 today is actually cheaper than $2,000 was in 1950.

It's important therefore, to analyze comparisons like this to be sure the statistics are indeed comparable. Any monetary comparisons need to take into consideration market value and inflation. When dealing with figures other than money there are other important concerns. For example, read the following argument:

> In 1990, there were 10 homicides in Boone County. In 2000, there were 25. That's an increase of 150% in just ten years. Crime in this country is becoming an epidemic!

What's wrong with this argument? Clearly, there has been a sharp rise in homicides in the last decade. But what the claim doesn't tell you is that during that same time period, the population of Boone County increased by 250%. Now how does that affect the argument?

If the population increased from 100,000 to 350,000, is the rise in homicides still evidence that can be used to support the claim "Crime in this country is becoming an epidemic"? No. In fact, this means that the number of homicides per capita (that is, per person) has actually decreased. Boone County is actually safer than it was. This is a case of comparing apples to oranges because the population in 1990 was so different than the population in 2000.

You should beware of any comparison across time, but the same problems can arise in contempo-rary comparisons. Take the following statistic, for example:

> Charleston Medical Center physicians perform more arthroscopic knee operations than St. Francis physicians, who use a technique that requires a large incision.

If you need to have knee surgery, should you go to Charleston Medical Center? Not necessarily. Consider this fact first: St. Francis physicians specialize in complicated knee surgeries that cannot be performed arthroscopically. Because their pool of patients is different from those of Charleston Medical Center, so will the number of nonarthroscopic knee operations differ.

Practice

Do the following statistics compare apples and or-anges, or are they fair comparisons?

7. I bought this house in 1964 for just $28,000. Now it's worth $130,000. What a profit I've made!

8. That shirt is $45. This one is only $15. They look exactly the same. I found a bargain!

9. The total crime rate for New City, when adjusted for population growth, rose 10% in the past year.

Answers

7. Apples and oranges. When this figure is adjusted for inflation, you might see that the house has the same market value.
8. This depends on what the shirts are made of. If they're both made of the same type and quality of material, then it's an apples to apples comparison. If, however, one shirt is made of silk and the other polyester, then it's apples and oranges.
9. Fair. It has been adjusted for population growth.

In Short

The truth about statistics is that they can be very misleading. When you come across statistics, check the source to see whether it's credible. Then find out the sample size and decide whether it's substantial enough. Look for evidence that the sample is representative of the population whose opinion you wish to reflect, or randomly selected and not biased. Finally, beware of statistics that compare apples to oranges by putting two unequal items side by side.

SKILL BUILDING UNTIL NEXT TIME

- Look for survey results in a reputable newspaper with a national circulation, like *The New York Times*, *Washington Post*, or *San Francisco Chronicle*. Notice how much information they provide about how the survey was conducted. Then, look for survey results in a tabloid or a less credible source. Notice how little information is provided and check for the possibility of bias.
- Think about a survey that you would like to conduct. Who is your target population? How would you ensure a representative sample? How large should your sample be?

20 ▶ Problem Solving Revisited

LESSON SUMMARY

Logic problems and puzzles can be fun, but they can also help determine the direction of your career if you ever have to take an exam that tests your logic and reasoning skills. This lesson shows you what types of questions you'll typically find on such an exam and how to tackle those kinds of questions.

Strong critical thinking and reasoning skills will help you make better decisions and solve problems more effectively on a day-to-day basis in your new career. But, equally as important, they'll also help you when you are taking the logic and reasoning skills section of your law enforcement entrance exam. Whatever the case, if you find yourself facing logic problems, you'll see they generally come in the form of questions that test your:

- common sense
- ability to distinguish good evidence from bad evidence
- ability to draw logical conclusions from evidence

You've been learning a lot about critical thinking and deductive and inductive reasoning, so you should already have the skills to tackle these kinds of questions. This lesson aims to familiarize you with the format of these kinds of test questions and to provide you with strategies for getting to the correct answer quickly.

Common Sense

Questions that test your common sense often present you with decision-making scenarios. Although the situation may be foreign to you and the questions may seem complicated, you can find the answer by remembering how to break a problem down into its parts and by thinking logically about the situation.

Sample Question

A police officer arrives at the scene of a two-car accident. In what order should the officer do the following?

1. Interview witnesses.
2. Determine whether anyone needs immediate medical attention.
3. Move the vehicles off of the roadway.
4. Interview the drivers to find out what happened.
   a. 2, 4, 3, 1
   b. 2, 4, 1, 3
   c. 2, 3, 1, 4
   d. 4, 2, 3, 1

The best answer is **b**, 2, 4, 1, 3. Your common sense should tell you that no matter what, the first priority is the safety of the people involved in the crash. That's why **2** has to come first on the list—and that means you can automatically eliminate answer **d**.

Now, again using your common sense, what should come next?

While statements from witnesses are important, it's more important to speak directly to the people involved in the accident, so **4** should follow **2**—and that eliminates answer **c**.

Now you're down to **a** and **b**. Why should you wait to move the vehicles off of the roadway? The main reason this doesn't come earlier is because you need to see the evidence—exactly where and how the cars ended up—as you listen to driver and wit-

ness testimony. Once you have their statements and have recorded the scene, *then* you can safely move the vehicles.

Practice

1. Using the previous scenario and, assuming that both drivers are in critical condition, write three things that the officer should do and the order in which he or she should do them.
   1. _____
   2. _____
   3. _____

Answer

Again, common sense should tell you that the first thing you need to do is get medical attention for the drivers. Number one on your list, then, should be *call an ambulance*. What next? Depending on the type of accident, the drivers may be in danger if they remain in the cars. Therefore, the next thing the officer should do is *quickly assess the damage to the cars* so that he or she can move the passengers to safety if there's a danger of an explosion. Finally, the police officer may not be a medic, but chances are he or she has some basic medical training. The next thing the police officer should do is *check to see if there's emergency care he or she can administer*. Perhaps the officer can administer CPR or bandage a badly bleeding wound until the ambulance arrives.

Remember, the key to answering this type of question is to remember how to prioritize issues, and that means you need to think carefully about many different possible scenarios.

Practice

2. C.O. Smith observes a fight break out in the mess hall. What should he do?
  I.   break up the fight
  II.   tend to the inmates' injuries
  III. notify other officers of the fight
  IV.   investigate what started the fight
  a. I, II, III, IV
  b. II, I, IV, III
  c. III, II, I, IV
  d. III, I, II, IV

Answer

The best answer is **d.** Without question, the first thing C.O. Smith needs to do is get help. He needs to call for assistance and let the other officers know that there is a problem. Once he has notified other officers and backup has arrived, C.O. Smith should attempt to stop the fight. Once the fight has ended, he should tend to any injuries. Finally, once everyone has been cared for and the situation is safe, he can begin the official investigation into the fight.

Evaluating Evidence

Law enforcement entrance exams often measure deductive as well as inductive reasoning skills. That's why some questions may ask you to evaluate evidence. Remember, strong evidence for a deductive argument is both *credible* and *reasonable*. You'll need to keep these criteria in mind and use your common sense to work your way through problems like the following sample question.

Sample Question

Defendants charged and found guilty of selling crack cocaine have filed suit in the Court of Appeals to have their sentences reduced. They are arguing that people who are found guilty of selling crack cocaine receive longer sentences than those found guilty of selling equal amounts of powder cocaine. Which of the following would provide the strongest support for their claim?

  a. People found guilty of selling crack cocaine and powder cocaine both have an average sentence of one year in prison per ounce sold.
  b. On average, people found guilty of selling crack cocaine serve twice the time in prison as do those selling equal amounts of powder cocaine.
  c. Ninety-four percent of prisoners incarcerated for selling crack cocaine agree with this argument.
  d. Joe sold two ounces of powder cocaine and received a sentence of two years. His brother sold two ounces of crack cocaine and received a sentence of one year.

You should have selected **b** as the answer. Why? Because **b** provides the most specific and relevant support for the argument. Though there is strength in numbers and it helps that 94% of prisoners incarcerated for selling crack cocaine agree (choice **c**, remember bias), the defendants are more likely to convince the court by providing concrete evidence. It's clear from the numbers provided in choice **b** that people who are found guilty of selling crack cocaine receive longer sentences than those found guilty of selling equal amounts of powder cocaine. Choice **a** actually disproves the argument as does choice **d**. Now it's your turn.

Practice

Read this scenario carefully and answer the questions that follow. City Council member Andrew Anderson claims that the city could save millions of dollars each year by turning services like garbage collection over to private companies.

3. Which of the following would provide the
strongest support for Anderson's argument?
- **a.** statistics showing how much the city spends
each year on these services
- **b.** statistics showing how much comparable
cities have saved by farming out these
services to private companies
- **c.** proposals from private companies showing
how well they could perform these services
for the city and at what costs
- **d.** a direct comparison of how much the city
spends per year on these services and how
much the city would save by farming the
services out to private companies

4. Which of the following is most likely to work
against Anderson's argument?
- **a.** statements from citizens protesting the
switch from public to private services
- **b.** statistics demonstrating how much more
the average citizen would have to pay for
privatization of these services
- **c.** reports from other cities with privatized
services about citizen protests that forced
the return to public services
- **d.** reports from other cities about corruption
among privatized service providers

Answers

3. The strongest support for Anderson's
argument is **d**, a direct comparison of how
much the city spends per year on these services
and how much the city would save by farming
the services out to private companies.
Remember, Anderson's argument is that the
city could save millions by turning these
services over to the private sector, and this
comparison would show exactly how much
this city (not other cities) would save.

4. Answer **c** is most likely to work against
Anderson's argument because it is the strongest
evidence that the plan didn't work in similar
cities. Furthermore, it shows that city councils
that had approved similar plans had to
reinstate public services due to citizen protests.
Since city council members are elected officials,
it's important for them to keep their con-
stituents happy, and **c** suggests privatizing these
services does not keep citizens happy.
Furthermore, you should be able to see that **a**,
b, and **d** are all reasons that would be likely to
cause citizens to protest and demand a return
to public services.

Drawing Conclusions from Evidence

Many questions you face when you're taking the logic
or reasoning skills section of your law enforcement
entrance exam will ask you to draw conclusions from
evidence. You've completed several lessons on inductive reasoning, so you should be quite good at these
questions, even if their format differs from what
you're used to. As with the other types of questions,
you can help ensure a correct response by using the
process of elimination. Given the evidence the question provides, you should automatically be able to
eliminate some of the answers.

Sample Question

A jeep has driven off the road and hit a tree. There are skid marks along the road for several yards leading up to a dead fawn. The marks then swerve to the right and off the road, stopping where the Jeep is. The impact with the tree is head-on, but the damage is not severe. Based on the evidence, which of the following is most likely what happened?

    a. The driver was aiming for the fawn and lost control of the Jeep.

    b. The driver fell asleep at the wheel and was awakened when he hit the fawn.

    c. The driver tried to avoid the fawn and lost control of the Jeep.

    d. The driver was drunk and out of control.

Given the facts—especially the key fact that there are skid marks—you can automatically eliminate choices **a** and **b**. If the driver were aiming for the fawn, he probably wouldn't have hit the brakes and created skid marks. Instead, he probably would have accelerated, in which case, his impact with the tree would have been harder and resulted in more damage. Similarly, if the driver had fallen asleep at the wheel and only awakened when he hit the fawn, there wouldn't have been skid marks leading up to the fawn.

So now you're down to two possibilities: **c** and **d**. Which is more likely to be true? While it is entirely possible that the driver was drunk, all the evidence points to **c** as the most likely possibility. The skid marks indicate that the driver was trying to stop to avoid hitting the fawn. Unsuccessful, he hit the animal and swerved off the road into a tree.

Other questions that ask you to draw conclusions from evidence may vary in format, but don't let their appearance throw you. If you read the following practice problems, for example, you'll see that you can tackle them quickly and easily by applying the evidence that's provided and eliminating the incorrect answers as you go along.

Practice

5. There are four brothers—Al, Bob, Carl, and Dave. Dave is two years older than Bob; Bob is one year younger than Carl; Al, who is 34, is two years younger than Carl. Which brother is oldest?
    a. Al
    b. Bob
    c. Carl
    d. Dave

6. Jack and Allison are planning the seating arrangements for their wedding reception. At one table are six guests. When deciding who should sit next to whom at this table, the couple has to keep in mind that:
- Guest 1 cannot sit next to Guest 2.
- Guests 3 and 4 must sit next to each other, but under no circumstances should Guest 4 sit next to Guest 1.
- Guest 5 can sit next to anyone except Guest 3.
- Guest 6 should not sit next to Guest 3 or 4 and would be happiest sitting next to Guest 5.

Which of the following is the best arrangement for this table?

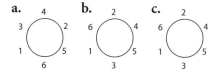

Answers

5. You can solve this puzzle easily by starting with this key fact: Al is 34 years old. Because you know Al's age, you can then determine that Carl is 36. That eliminates Al as the oldest. Then from Carl's age, you can determine that Bob is 35; that eliminates Bob, too. From Bob's age, you can determine that Dave is 37. That makes Dave the oldest and **d** the correct answer. It may also help to chart out the relationship placing the oldest at the top of your list and then filling in the rest.

6. Though the question seems complicated, the answer is really quite simply achieved. Start with this key piece of information—3 and 4 must sit next to each other and 4 cannot sit with 1. Why is this the key piece? Because it allows you to seat three of the six guests immediately. Then the other three should easily fall into place and you can see that choice **a** is the correct answer. Again charting the relationships out may help you to solve this problem.

In Short

Tests that aim to measure your critical thinking and reasoning skills generally ask three types of questions: those that measure your common sense, those that measure your ability to recognize good evidence, and those that measure your ability to draw logical conclusions from evidence. You'll perform well on these tests if you remember to break down the parts of a problem and think about different possible scenarios, keep in mind the criteria for strong arguments and good evidence, and start inductive reasoning questions by working with the key facts. Use the process of elimination to help you arrive at the correct answer.

SKILL BUILDING UNTIL NEXT TIME

- Stop in your local bookstore or go to the library and get a book of logic problems and puzzles. The more you practice them, the better you'll get at solving them.
- Write your own logic problems and puzzles. Test them on your family and friends. Be sure you can clearly explain the correct answer.

21 ▶ Putting It All Together

LESSON SUMMARY

This lesson puts together the strategies and skills you've learned throughout this book, particularly in Lessons 11 through 20. You'll review the key points of these lessons and practice both your inductive and deductive reasoning skills.

Before you begin putting it all together, let's review what you've learned in the second half of this book. If you'd like a quick review of the first half, turn to Lesson 10.

Lesson 11: Logical Fallacies: Appeals to Emotion

You learned that people will often try to convince you to accept their claims by appealing to your emotions rather than to your sense of reason. They may use *scare tactics*, *flattery*, or *peer pressure*, or they may appeal to your *sense of pity*.

Lesson 12: Logical Fallacies: The Impostors

You learned about four logical fallacies that pretend to be logical but don't hold water. *No in-betweens* claims that there are only two choices when, in fact, there are many. The *slippery slope* fallacy argues that if *X* happens, then *Y* will follow, even though *X* doesn't necessarily lead to *Y*. *Circular reasoning* is an argument that goes in a circle—the premises simply restate the conclusion. And *two wrongs make a right* argues that it's okay to do something to someone else because someone else might do something bad to you.

Lesson 13: Logical Fallacies: Distracters and Distorters

You learned how to recognize three common logical fallacies that divert your attention and distort the issue. An *ad hominem* fallacy attacks the *person* instead of attacking the claims that that person makes. A *red herring* distracts you by bringing in an irrelevant issue, while the *straw man* distorts the opponent's position so that the opponent is easier to knock down.

Lesson 14: Making Judgment Calls

You learned how to reason through arguments and evaluate evidence. Now it is time to take action. Making judgment calls is an important part of critical thinking. You learned that you need to consider any facts you can gather, the advice of others, your intuition, and even your values. Take your time with judgment calls, and with practice, you will become more confident in making them.

Lesson 15: Why Did It Happen?

You practiced evaluating explanations for validity. You learned that explanations must be relevant and testable and that you should reject explanations that are circular. You also learned the importance of being wary of explanations that contradict your existing knowledge or accepted theories.

Lesson 16: Inductive Reasoning

You learned that inductive reasoning is the process of drawing logical conclusions from evidence. You also learned that a good inductive argument is one in which it is very *likely* that the premises lead to the conclusion.

Lesson 17: Jumping to Conclusions

You learned to distinguish between good inductive reasoning and inductive fallacies like *hasty generalizations*, which draw conclusions from too little evidence. *Biased generalizations* draw conclusions from biased evidence, and *non sequiturs* draw conclusions that don't logically follow from the premises.

Lesson 18: More Inductive Reasoning

You learned the two inductive reasoning approaches to determining cause: looking for what's different and looking for the common denominator. You learned to look for other possible differences and common causes and to watch out for the *post hoc, ergo propter hoc* fallacy assuming that because *A* came before *B*, *A* caused *B*. You also learned how to avoid the *chicken or egg* causal argument.

Lesson 19: Numbers Never Lie

You learned that numbers can be very misleading. You practiced checking statistics for a *reliable source*, an adequate *sample size*, and a *representative sample*. You also learned how to recognize statistics that compare apples and oranges.

Lesson 20: Problem Solving Revisited

You put your critical thinking and deductive and inductive reasoning skills to work on the kind of questions you might find on a logic or reasoning skills exam. You solved logic problems designed to test your common sense, ability to recognize good evidence, and ability to draw logical conclusions from evidence.

> If any of these terms or strategies sound unfamiliar to you, STOP. Take a few minutes to review whatever lessons remain unclear.

Practice

Let's utilize the skills that we have covered in this book to answer typical reasoning questions found on various law enforcement entrance exams. These questions are examples of the types of critical thinking/logical reasoning questions that you will encounter on police, probations, corrections, and federal law enforcement entrance exams. Make every attempt to simulate a real-life testing environment. Find a quiet space and time yourself. Good luck.

Select the most appropriate answer that follows each question.

1. Naturalized U.S. citizens can lose their U.S. citizenship if and only if they expatriate or are denaturalized. Misrepresentation on a legal permanent residence application, certain crimes, and leaving the United States within one year of naturalization to establish permanent residence elsewhere are all grounds for denaturalization. P.C. is a naturalized U.S. citizen. *From the information given, it can be validly concluded that*
   a. if P.C. loses her U.S. citizenship without being denaturalized, then she must have expatriated.
   b. if P.C. does not expatriate, then she cannot lose her U.S. citizenship.
   c. if P.C. is denaturalized, then she must have made a misrepresentation on her legal permanent residence application.
   d. if P.C. has committed no crimes, then she cannot be denaturalized.
   e. P.C. cannot lose her U.S. citizenship without being denaturalized.

2. Following the Vietnam War, many people from Southeast Asia were paroled into the United States with an indefinite immigration status. In 2003, a new rule was developed to allow for adjustment of immigration status for some of these people. According to the new rule, all nationals of Vietnam (and some others—for example, nationals of Cambodia) who were paroled into the United States through the Orderly Departure Program were eligible to apply for permanent resident status. *From the information given, it can be validly concluded that*, based on the new rule of 2003,

- **a.** everyone eligible to apply for permanent resident status is a national of Vietnam who was paroled into the United States through the Orderly Departure Program.
- **b.** no one ineligible to apply for permanent resident status was a national of Vietnam who was paroled into the United States through the Orderly Departure Program.
- **c.** only nationals of Vietnam who were paroled into the United States through the Orderly Departure Program were eligible to apply for permanent resident status.
- **d.** some nationals of Vietnam who were paroled into the United States through the Orderly Departure Program were ineligible to apply for permanent resident status.
- **e.** some of those who were ineligible to apply for permanent resident status were nationals of Vietnam who were paroled into the United States through the Orderly Departure Program.

3. An employer is permitted to hire a new employee only if the employer is able to verify that the applicant's employment documentation establishes both of the following: (1) The applicant is authorized to work in the United States; (2) the applicant who presents the employment authorization document is the person to whom the documentation was issued. An employer cannot request that an applicant provide more or different documents than required. If the documentation appears false or unrelated, employers must refuse acceptance and ask for other documentation from the government's list of acceptable documents. *From the information given, it CANNOT be validly concluded that*

- **a.** no employer is permitted to limit which documents it will accept for verification of employment authorization.
- **b.** if an employer cannot verify that an applicant is authorized to work, then the employer is not permitted to hire the applicant.
- **c.** if an applicant's documentation appears to be true and relevant to an employer, the employer must refuse acceptance and ask for other documentation from the government's list of acceptable documents.
- **d.** an employer may request different employment documentation if the provided documentation appears to be altered.
- **e.** if an applicant is permitted to be hired, then the applicant has verifiable employment authorization.

4. In a certain border state, all state peace officers have the authority to issue state citations for misdemeanor marijuana and paraphernalia offenses committed in their presence. Early last year, a certain border patrol sector in the state began a new operation with state police. Under this operation, all sector canine handlers were cross-designated as state peace officers. *From the information given, it CANNOT be validly concluded that, in the border state discussed,*

   a. at least some law enforcement officers who can issue citations for misdemeanor marijuana and paraphernalia offenses committed in their presence are state peace officers.

   b. all sector canine handlers have the authority to issue state citations for misdemeanor marijuana and paraphernalia offenses committed in their presence.

   c. at least some individuals who have the authority to issue citations for misdemeanor marijuana and paraphernalia offenses committed in their presence are sector canine handlers.

   d. no sector canine handlers lack the authority to issue state citations for misdemeanor marijuana and paraphernalia offenses committed in their presence.

   e. only sector canine handlers have the authority to issue citations for misdemeanor marijuana and paraphernalia offenses committed in their presence.

5. Green cards authorize aliens to work in the United States. The cards have a ten-year expiration period. Application for a renewal of a green card can be made beginning six months in advance of expiration. In order to apply for renewal of a green card, the applicant is required to apply in person and bring his or her current green card, application, fee, and new photos. It may take one year for applicants to receive new green cards, but temporary documents are provided. *From the information given, it CANNOT be validly concluded that*

   a. an application that does not require the applicant to apply in person cannot be a renewal application for a green card.

   b. application for a replacement green card cannot be made more than six months in advance of expiration.

   c. green cards are the only work authorization documents that expire after ten years.

   d. it is not the case that some green cards never expire.

   e. some renewed green cards are not available in less than one year.

6. Inmates should be watched closely for signs of behavioral changes, because some inmates develop problems that lead to suicide attempts. Officer Bettis knows his inmates well. Which of the following situations should cause him concern?

a. Inmate Fredericks is withdrawn and depressed. He hardly eats and has told other inmates that his wife wrote him a letter telling him she never wants to see him again.

b. Early one morning, inmate Edwards decides he is not hungry and is not going to line up with the other inmates to report for breakfast.

c. Inmates Jardin and Lipscomb argue constantly whenever they are around each other. Inmate Jardin says he thinks Lipscomb is an idiot.

d. Last week, inmate Hass was injured in a fight and now has his jaws wired shut. He sits in his cell and doesn't speak to the other inmates.

Use the following information to answer questions 7 through 11.

Officers frequently handle domestic disturbance calls. Since these calls are dangerous for both the families involved and the officers, officers called to the scene of a domestic disturbance should carry out the following nine steps in the order listed:

1. Inform the dispatcher when they arrive.
2. Park the patrol car away from the residence.
3. Before knocking, listen carefully at the door to get an idea of what is happening inside.
4. Stand on either side of the door while knocking, in order to be less vulnerable to gunshots or immediate attack.
5. Knock and identify themselves as police officers.
6. Once inside, restore order as calmly as possible by separating those who are arguing.
7. Administer first aid if immediately necessary.
8. Talk to the participants separately and find out what happened.
9. Let the dispatcher know if the situation is under control or if assistance is needed.

7. Officers Charles and Washington have been dispatched to 2104 Maple Avenue. Neighbors called 911 and said that they could hear Jeff threatening his wife Sara and that they were afraid he was about to beat her. Officer Charles notifies the dispatcher that they have arrived. He parks the car in front of 2102 Maple, and he and Officer Washington begin walking up the sidewalk to 2104 Maple Ave. What should the two officers do next?

a. Knock on the front door and request entry.

b. Listen at the door to see if they can tell what is going on inside.

c. Talk to the neighbors who called before taking any action.

d. Administer first aid to those who are injured.

8. Officer Wallace arrives at the scene of a domestic disturbance. After notifying the dispatcher of her arrival and parking her car a few houses away, Officer Wallace is at the house's front door. She listens for a few minutes and hears a woman sobbing. The house is dark and quiet except for the sounds of the woman crying. The next step Officer Wallace should take is to
   a. walk around to the rear of the house and listen at the back door.
   b. knock on the door and identify herself.
   c. call to the woman through the door to ask if she is injured.
   d. step to one side of the door before knocking.

9. Officers Stanley and DiMartino have just pulled up to the curb near 9000 Block Parkway on a domestic disturbance call. Neighbors are reporting sounds of breaking glass, yelling, and gunshots. What is the first thing the officers should do?
   a. Listen at the door to see if they can tell what is happening.
   b. Get the dispatcher to have a neighbor meet them outside to tell them what they heard.
   c. Radio in to the dispatcher when they arrive at the scene.
   d. Immediately run into the residence.

10. Officer Roberts is dispatched to a domestic disturbance at 3412 Runnymeade. When he arrives, he radios in to the dispatcher and parks at 3410 Runnymeade. As he approaches the house, the door flies open and a woman runs out. She is bleeding heavily from a cut on her arm and collapses at his feet, crying, "Help me, officer!" The next thing Officer Roberts should do is to
   a. apply first aid to the woman's wound.
   b. search the house for the suspect.
   c. separate the victim and the suspect.
   d. identify himself to the victim.

11. "He's got almost all of the credentials we are looking for, but I don't think we should hire him—he's a vegetarian."
   a. The speaker is committing the *ad hominem* fallacy.
   b. The speaker is presenting the chicken or egg dilemma.
   c. This is a *post hoc* fallacy.
   d. There's nothing wrong with the speaker's reasoning.

12. Four police officers are chasing a suspect on foot. Officer Calvin is directly behind the suspect. Partners Jenkins and Burton are side by side behind Calvin. Officer Zeller is behind Jenkins and Burton. Burton trips and falls, and Calvin turns back to help him. An officer tackles the suspect. Which officer caught the suspect?
   a. Burton
   b. Zeller
   c. Jenkins
   d. Calvin

13. Officers Roberts and Reed are on bicycle patrol in the downtown area. Sergeant McElvey tells them that a white male has been committing robberies along the nearby bike path by stepping out of the bushes and threatening bicyclists with an iron pipe until they give him their bicycles. There have been three separate incidents, and the suspect descriptions are from three different victims.

Robbery #1: Suspect is a white male, 20–25 years old, 5′9″, 145 pounds, with a shaved head, wearing a skull earring in the left ear, floppy white T-shirt, worn light blue jeans, and black combat boots.

Robbery #2: Suspect is a white male, 25–30 years old, dark brown hair in a military-style crew cut, 6′2″, 200 pounds, wearing a white T-shirt with the words "Just Do It" on the back, blue surgical scrub pants, and black combat boots.

Robbery #3: Suspect is a white male, 23 years old, 5′10″, skinny build, no hair, wearing a tie-dyed T-shirt, blue baggy pants, dark shoes, and one earring.

Three days after Sergeant McElvey told the officers about the robberies, Officer Reed arrests a suspect for attempting to take a woman's mountain bike from her on the bicycle path. The description of the suspect is as follows:

Robbery #4: Suspect is a white male, 22 years old, 140 pounds, 5′10″, with a shaved head and one pierced ear, wearing a plain white T-shirt two sizes too large for him, faded baggy blue jeans, and scuffed black combat boots. After comparing the suspect description with those in the first three robberies, in which of the other robberies should Officer Reed consider the arrested man a suspect?

a. Robbery #1, Robbery #2, and Robbery #3
b. Robbery #1, but not Robbery #2 or Robbery #3
c. Robbery #1 and Robbery #3, but not Robbery #2
d. Robbery #1 and Robbery #2, but not Robbery #3

14. Officer Troy arrives at the scene of a hit-and-run traffic accident. Ms. Chen tells him she was waiting for the light to change when a car struck her from behind. The driver backed up and left the scene. She saw his license plate as he left, as did three teenaged witnesses waiting for the school bus. The choices below list what each one reported. Which license plate number below is most likely the license plate of the hit-and-run vehicle?
a. JXK 12L
b. JYK 12L
c. JXK 12I
d. JXX I2L

15. Four eyewitnesses give descriptions of the getaway car used in a bank robbery. Which description is probably right?
a. dark blue with a white roof
b. dark green with a gray roof
c. black with a gray roof
d. dark green with a tan roof

16. Law enforcement agencies use scientific techniques to identify suspects or to establish guilt. One obvious application of such techniques is the examination of a crime scene. Some substances found at a crime scene yield valuable clues under microscopic examination. Clothing fibers, dirt particles, and even pollen grains may reveal important information to the careful investigator. Nothing can be overlooked, because all substances found at a crime scene are potential sources of evidence. *From the information given, it can be validly concluded that*

a. all substances that yield valuable clues under microscopic examination are substances found at a crime scene.

b. some potential sources of evidence are substances that yield valuable clues under microscopic examination.

c. some substances found at a crime scene are not potential sources of evidence.

d. no potential sources of evidence are substances found at a crime scene.

e. some substances that yield valuable clues under microscopic examination are not substances found at a crime scene.

17. Immigrants may try to enter the United States illegally for a variety of reasons. Among these reasons are to get jobs they hope will improve their financial situation, to reunite with family members in the United States, and to find political freedom. There's ongoing debate in the United States about how many immigrants should be admitted and under what conditions. Meanwhile, smugglers known as coyotes take advantage of the situation by collecting thousands of dollars from those wishing to cross the border illegally. For their money, immigrants often endure days or even weeks of unpleasant conditions and no guarantees of success or even survival. *From the information given, it can be validly concluded that*

a. smugglers charge too much money for the services they provide.

b. illegal immigrants sometimes risk their lives to enter the United States with no guarantees.

c. illegal immigrants are never successfully integrated into U.S. society.

d. illegal immigrants always improve their financial situation in the United States.

e. debating about immigration levels will eventually result in protecting more illegal immigrants from coyotes.

18. Border patrol agents are sometimes required to testify in court about their activities leading up to and during an arrest. Therefore, agents must have excellent communication skills. They need to be able to express themselves clearly in court and elsewhere so they are understood without confusion or misinterpretation. By their choice of words and how they speak, they must demonstrate to a judge or jury that they are confident and capable. A public speaking course would be an excellent way for agents to ensure that they're making the best possible impression in court. *From the information given, it can be validly concluded that*

   a. excellent communication skills are important only when an agent is in court.

   b. excellent communication skills are essential for all border patrol agents.

   c. no agents would benefit from a public speaking course.

   d. trained public speakers would make excellent border patrol agents.

   e. an agent's choice of words and confidence have little effect on a judge or jury.

19. The printed output of some computer-driven printers can be recognized by forensic analysts. The Acme Model 200 printer was manufactured using two different inking mechanisms, one of which yields a Type A micro pattern of ink spray around its characters. Of all Acme Model 200 printers, 70% produce this Type A micro pattern, which is also characteristic of some models of other printers. Forensic analysts at a crime lab have been examining a falsified document that clearly exhibits the Type A micro pattern. *From the information given, it can be validly concluded that* this document

   a. was printed on an Acme Model 200 printer, with a probability of 70%.

   b. was printed on an Acme Model 200 printer, with a probability of 30%.

   c. was not printed on an Acme Model 200 printer, with a probability of 70%.

   d. was not printed on an Acme Model 200 printer, with a probability of 30%.

   e. may have been printed on an Acme Model 200 printer, but the probability cannot be estimated.

20. Quite often, a border patrol agent is required to give assistance to an injured person. Upon responding to a call to assist an injured person, an agent should be guided by the following procedure:

- administer first aid
- call for medical assistance
- call the ambulance again if it fails to arrive within 20 minutes
- accompany the injured person to the hospital if he or she is unidentified or unconscious
- witness a search of an unidentified or unconscious person
- attempt to identify an unconscious person by searching belongings

While on patrol, Agent Maguire observes a man lying ten yards from the international boundary in Imperial Beach, CA. When questioned, the man reveals he fell while scaling the border fence. He claims he is in a great deal of pain and is unable to move. Agent Maguire requests an ambulance and provides immediate first aid. He then asks the man his name. However, the man refuses to answer. The ambulance arrives in 15 minutes when a supervisory border patrol agent guides it to the remote area. Agent Maguire resumes his normal patrol duties immediately east of the area. *From the information given, it can be validly concluded that* Agent Maguire failed to fulfill his obligations in this incident because he

a. did not make a second call for the ambulance when the man was in great pain.

b. failed to accompany the man to the hospital.

c. did not attempt to locate a doctor while waiting for the ambulance.

d. failed to relieve the injured man's pain through proper first aid.

e. failed to notify a supervisory border patrol agent.

21. Visa regulations allow employers in certain industries to hire foreign nationals for seasonal positions. These employers must first try to hire U.S. workers for these positions. Eligible industries include landscaping, seasonal hospitality and seasonal construction, and certain jobs in manufacturing, food packaging and processing, fisheries, and retail. Agriculture is not an eligible industry. Workers must return to their home countries at the end of the season. The program benefits both employers who need workers and foreigners who need the income. *From the information given, it can be validly concluded that*

a. foreign workers in all industries are eligible for seasonal position visas.

b. no U.S. workers are eligible for any seasonal positions.

c. a foreign worker wanting to work on a farm would not be eligible for a seasonal visa.

d. only seasonal position visas are available to foreign workers in agriculture.

e. all manufacturing jobs are available to foreigners with seasonal visas.

22. One way that a foreign national is eligible to become a lawful permanent resident of the United States is by being sponsored by a relative. The relative must be able to prove that he or she is a citizen of the United States and must demonstrate that he or she can support the foreign national at 125% above the mandated poverty line. In addition, if the relative is a U.S. citizen, then he or she may sponsor a husband or wife, unmarried children under 21, married son or daughter of any age, brother or sister (if the sponsor is at least 21), or parent (if the sponsor is at least 21). *From the information given, it can be validly concluded that*

a. if a sponsoring relative is a U.S. citizen, he or she may sponsor a husband or wife regardless of age.

b. there is no financial requirement for a U.S. citizen to sponsor a son or daughter under 21.

c. the only way that a foreign national is eligible to become a lawful permanent resident of the United States is by being sponsored by a relative.

d. the best way that a foreign national is eligible to become a lawful permanent resident of the United States is by being sponsored by a relative.

e. a U.S. citizen may sponsor a brother or sister only if the foreign national meets the age requirements.

23. The Immigration and Nationality Act (INA) provides for naturalization, the process by which a foreign citizen or national can become a U.S. citizen. Some of the requirements are continuous residence and physical presence in the United States; an ability to read, write, and speak English; a knowledge and understanding of U.S. history and government; and favorable disposition toward the United States. *From the information given, it can be validly concluded that*

a. a foreign national who speaks only French might be eligible for naturalization.

b. a foreign national with very limited understanding of U.S. history might be eligible for naturalization.

c. without a favorable disposition toward the United States, a foreign national cannot be naturalized.

d. a foreign national who cannot read English can be naturalized under certain circumstances.

e. a foreign national arriving in the United States today can become naturalized next week under certain circumstances.

24. Grounds for deportation of aliens fall into two broad categories. The first covers prohibited acts committed at or prior to entry into the United States (which includes having entered the country illegally—for example, by falsifying documents or evading inspection at the border). The second covers prohibited acts committed since entry into the United States (for example, committing a criminal offense or engaging in activity whose purpose is the overthrow of the U.S. government by force). In regard to the former category, the Immigration and Nationality Act permits the Department of Homeland Security (DHS) to look back and deport aliens who should not have been admitted in the first place, had their prohibited acts been known. *From the information given, it can be validly concluded that*

a. only aliens who have committed a deportable offense prior to entering the United States may be deported.

b. some aliens who have not committed a deportable offense prior to entering the United States may be deported.

c. aliens may be deported only if they commit prohibited acts both before and after entering the United States.

d. only aliens who have falsified documents or evaded inspection of the border may be deported.

e. only aliens who have committed criminal acts or advocated the overthrow of the U.S. government by force may be deported.

25. The U.S. Supreme Court has consistently held that the decision to admit an alien to the United States or to exclude an alien from the United States lies entirely with Congress and that Congress can set whatever terms it chooses. Congress has the authority to discriminate on the basis of nationality, race, political belief, moral character, or mental or physical disability. In addition, Congress can grant special preference to relatives of U.S. residents, and to persons possessing work skills that would tend to boost the U.S. economy. However, once admitted to the United States, aliens can claim most of the protections guaranteed by the Constitution—for example, freedom of speech and religion, freedom from unreasonable search and seizure—but not the right to hold federal elective office. People who are undergoing proceedings to expel them from the United States are likewise granted the safeguards of due process under the Fifth Amendment and cannot be compelled to incriminate themselves. *From the information given, it CANNOT be validly concluded that*

a. a person seeking to enter the United States has virtually no legal rights.

b. a person, once admitted to the United States, cannot hold any elected office.

c. some noncitizens are guaranteed certain constitutional rights, even if they engage in criminal activities.

d. people pending deportation have a right to due process without regard to the opinion Congress may hold of that person.

e. a person seeking to enter the United States can be excluded on the basis of nationality or race.

26. In recent years, as few as 5,200 border patrol agents have apprehended a million or more illegal aliens per year. Agents routinely work alone, often arresting 20 or more aliens at one time without assistance. They often work in riot conditions, and encounter terrorists and violent gang members. The job often requires physical exertion under difficult environmental conditions. *From the information given, it can be validly concluded that*

 a. working closely and well with a partner is a key element of being a border patrol agent.

 b. being able to think fast while working alone is important to being a successful border patrol agent.

 c. being a border patrol agent involves apprehending illegal aliens exclusively.

 d. border patrol activities are generally suspended during bad weather.

 e. being in good physical condition is of little importance for border patrol agents.

27. The Border Patrol sets out to protect U.S. borders by simultaneously focusing on five key strategies: apprehending terrorists and terrorist weapons illegally entering the United States; deterring illegal entries through improved enforcement; detecting, apprehending, and deterring smugglers of humans, drugs, and other contraband; using smart border technology; and reducing crime in border communities, thereby improving quality of life. Agents are trained to understand each of these areas, and need to be ready on short notice to implement any or all of these strategies. *From the information given, it can be validly concluded that* border patrol agents

 a. never prevent illegal aliens from entering the country, but focus on apprehending them after they arrive.

 b. always give priority to apprehending terrorists, not smugglers.

 c. always give priority to apprehending smugglers, not terrorists.

 d. must focus on several strategies simultaneously to secure U.S. borders.

 e. always reduce crime in border communities as a first step toward securing our borders.

28. In August 2008, U.S. and Mexican officials spoke of increased cooperation between their countries to try to reduce drug smuggling across the border. "We are destroying the crime organizations' structure, and that has spurred more violence . . . as the drug organizations spread out to kidnapping and extortion to make money," said Manuel Suárez-Mier, legal attaché for the Mexican attorney general. "What we need is the full commitment of the United States, particularly in helping integrate technology we don't have access to. . . . "We are seeing the benefits of greater cooperation between the United States and Mexico, but the price has been high for us," he said. "More than 2,500 people have been killed in the drug wars, and people want immediate results." Michael Sullivan, director of the U.S. Bureau of Alcohol, Tobacco, Firearms and Explosives, said, "We have asked Mexico to assist in stopping the flow of drugs across our borders, and they have done so extraordinarily well—and at great cost to civilians and law enforcement officers targeted for execution and assassinations by the drug cartels. What Mexico asks us to do is something similar, to halt the flow of guns into Mexico." *From the information given, it can validly be concluded that*

a. the U.S. and Mexican governments are frustrated by the lack of cooperation between the two countries.

b. progress is slow, and drug dealers are more successful than ever in bringing drugs across the border.

c. Mexico's efforts to limit drug traffic have been stalled.

d. Mexico has paid a price for trying to reduce drug traffic, but continued cooperation between the countries is expected to yield results over time.

e. Mexico is completely responsible for increased drug traffic and lack of technology that could improve the situation.

29. A-1 and A-2 visas to the United States are valid for as long as the secretary of state extends recognition to the holder. A-3 visas are valid for not more than three years but may be extended in increments of not more than two years. In 2008, A-1 visas are given to Adara Janus, her husband, and their two children, because Adara is an ambassador from her country. At the same time, an A-3 visa is given to Oden Wolf, Adara's personal assistant. Also in 2008, an A-2 visa is given to Hedrick Yuli, an employee of his country's government, and an A-3 visa is given to Ron Tripp, Hedrick's personal secretary. *From the information given, it can be validly concluded that,* if Hedrick asks Ron Tripp to remain in the United States for nine years, until the year 2017, Ron

a. could not do this because his visa is valid for only three years.

b. could not do this because his visa is valid for only five years (three years plus an extension of two years).

c. could do this as long as the secretary of state extended recognition to him.

d. could do this if he were granted three more two-year extensions.

e. could do this because of a request by his employer.

30. Although undercover work by the police or by government officials is allowed, it has limitations. For example, if an officer or agent of the government induces a person to commit a crime that the person has not contemplated committing, for the purpose of instituting criminal prosecution against that person, this is called entrapment and is illegal. Entrapment can occur in two ways: (1) by knowingly representing the crime in a false light, so that it will not be seen by the person as illegal; and (2) by employing persuasive tactics that will induce the person to commit the illegal act when that person originally had no intention of committing it. *From the information given, it can be validly concluded that*, if an undercover officer named Ron arrests a suspect named Sheryl for an act they have discussed beforehand,

a. Ron is not guilty of entrapment unless Sheryl was not intending to commit the crime until Ron suggested it.

b. Ron is guilty of entrapment if he suggested that the crime was not illegal, and Sheryl was already intending to commit it.

c. Sheryl is not the victim of entrapment if she was not intending to commit the crime until Ron suggested it.

d. Sheryl is not the victim of entrapment if she committed the crime suggested by Ron because he said it was not illegal.

e. Ron is not guilty of entrapment if he suggested committing a crime and Sheryl did it without contemplating it beforehand.

31. A U.S. citizen can lose his or her citizenship in one of two ways, by denaturalization (which applies to naturalized citizens only) or by expatriation (which can apply to both naturalized citizens and citizens by birth). Denaturalization takes place when a court revokes the naturalization order because it is found to have been illegally or fraudulently obtained. Expatriation takes place when any citizen voluntarily abandons his or her country and becomes a citizen or subject of another. The Supreme Court has said, however, that the expatriate must have voluntarily performed an expatriating act in order for loss of citizenship to occur (for example, becoming a citizen of another country, serving in the military of a hostile country, or formally renouncing nationality before a diplomatic officer of the United States). *From the information given, it can be validly concluded that*

a. no denaturalization takes place if the naturalization order is found not to have been obtained legally.

b. expatriation takes place only if the act of expatriating is not involuntary.

c. no expatriation takes place if the act of expatriating is voluntary.

d. no denaturalization takes place unless the naturalization order is found to have been obtained legally.

e. expatriation takes place unless the act of expatriating is not involuntary.

32. Officer Yang has noticed an increase in gang graffiti in his area. Store owners are complaining about the damage and have asked him to keep a closer eye out for this problem. Which situation should Officer Yang investigate?

   a. Two teenagers are leaning against a park wall completely covered with gang-related graffiti.

   b. Four teenagers are leaning against the clean white wall of a neighborhood grocery store. One teenager has a spray paint can hanging out of the rear pocket of his pants.

   c. Three teenagers are riding bicycles in a grocery store parking lot late at night.

   d. Six teenagers are walking along the sidewalk bouncing a basketball and yelling at passing cars while making gang signs with their hands.

33. Shoplifting is a theft of goods from a store, shop, or place of business during business hours where the suspect takes the good(s) past the last point of opportunity to pay for the merchandise without attempting to offer payment. Which of the following is the best example of shoplifting?

   a. Terry walks into the Bag and Save grocery store and gets a piece of candy. He takes it to the counter and discovers he has no money. The clerk tells him to go ahead and keep the candy this time. Terry leaves the store eating the candy.

   b. Gloria walks into an electronics store to get a pack of triple-A batteries. She sticks the small package in her coat pocket while she looks at the computer display. After a few minutes, she turns to walk out. Before she reaches the door, she remembers the batteries and turns back to the counter to pay for them.

   c. Gail enters Philo's Pharmacy on 12th Street to pick up a prescription. After paying for the medicine, she walks over to the perfume counter, where she finds a small bottle of cologne she likes. She puts the cologne in her purse and walks out the front door of the pharmacy.

   d. Pete and his mother, Abby, are grocery shopping. Pete picks up a candy bar, peels off the wrapper, and hands Abby the wrapper. When they reach the checkout counter, Pete walks out of the store while Abby puts the groceries, along with the candy wrapper, on the stand for checkout. The clerk rings up the price of the candy along with the groceries.

Use the following information to answer questions 34 through 36.

The use of warnings may sometimes provide a satisfactory solution to a problem and may enhance the public perception of the department. Normally, the use of a warning occurs in traffic offenses, but warnings may occasionally be applied to misdemeanor criminal offenses. In determining whether a warning should be issued, the officer should consider:

1. the seriousness of the offense
2. the likelihood that the violator will heed the warning
3. the reputation of the violator, (i.e., known repeat offender, has received previous warnings, etc.)

34. Which of the following is the best example of a situation in which a police officer might issue a warning?
   a. a city councilperson who has been stopped for drunk driving
   b. a known heroin addict who is trespassing in an abandoned building
   c. a group of 14-year-old boys who are throwing rocks at each other
   d. a 35-year-old woman on probation for shoplifting who has been detained for stealing $2 from a local store

35. Which of the following is a situation where a police officer could NOT issue a warning?
   a. a minor traffic violation
   b. a ten-year-old who shoplifted a candy bar
   c. a felony assault
   d. a city councilperson accused of trespassing

36. Which of the following is the best situation for a police officer to issue a warning?
   a. a foreign tourist accused of stealing $500
   b. a 22-year-old soldier, home on leave, who is drunk in public
   c. an offender who has a warrant for failing to appear in court
   d. a 35-year-old man with an out-of-state driver's license who is accused of fraud

37. Extortion is a less serious crime than burglary. Breaking and entering is more serious than extortion, but less serious than assault. Assault is more serious than burglary. Which crime is the most serious?
   a. burglary
   b. breaking and entering
   c. assault
   d. extortion

Use the following information to answer questions 38 through 40.

After arresting a suspect, officers should conduct a search for weapons and contraband by doing the following:

1. Make sure the prisoner's hands are handcuffed securely behind his or her back.
2. Check the waistband and area within reach of the prisoner's handcuffed hands.
3. Check the prisoner's cap or hat.
4. Check the neck area and both arms.
5. Check the prisoner's front pockets.
6. Check the inseam of the pants and crotch area.
7. Check the legs and ankles.
8. Check the prisoner's shoes.

38. Officer Linder arrests a man wearing a baseball cap, a T-shirt, blue jeans, and lace-up work boots. She checks to make sure the handcuffs are secure. She notices a bulge in his cap. What should Officer Linder do next?
a. Check his front pockets.
b. Check the cap for weapons.
c. Check the prisoner's waistband.
d. Check the area near his neck.

39. Officer Petrochowsky arrests a man for public intoxication. The man is wearing a cowboy hat, a long-sleeved shirt, dress slacks, and cowboy boots. The officer checks the prisoner's handcuffs and checks to make sure the waistband and back pocket area are clear of weapons. Suddenly, the prisoner sits down on the curb and refuses to stand up. Two other officers help get the prisoner to his feet. What should Officer Petrochowsky do next?
a. Check the prisoner's cowboy hat.
b. Check the prisoner's boots.
c. Check the prisoner's waistband and back pocket area.
d. Take the prisoner straight to jail before he tries to sit back down.

40. Officer Chastaine has a woman under arrest for possession of cocaine. She is wearing a scarf, a long dress, stockings, and high heels. He checks to make sure the handcuffs are secure on the woman. What should he do next?
a. Check the suspect's scarf.
b. Check the waistline of the suspect's dress and any pockets near her hands.
c. Check the suspect's neck area.
d. Check the suspect's shoes, which are partially hidden by her skirt.

Use the following information to answer questions 41 through 47.

Henry Allen, fiscally conservative candidate for city council, contacted the Internal Security Division of the Internal Revenue Service and alleged that an IRS employee was giving Allen's tax information to an opponent, Susan Vickers. Vickers was threatening to release information that Allen's business had been operating at a loss for five years. Molly Hepplewhite, an internal security inspector for the IRS, commences an investigation. During the course of the investigation, the following statements were made.

1. Milton Banks, Susan Vickers's neighbor, said that he once caught Vickers going through his trash.
2. Bill Pushman, Henry Allen's campaign manager, said that he dated Alice West in college. Alice now works at the IRS.
3. Shelby Gray, Susan Vickers's sister, said that Susan would always do whatever she needed to do to get what she wanted.
4. Calvin Morris, Susan Vickers's campaign manager, said that his sister-in-law, Mary Yate, works at the IRS, but they haven't spoken in months.
5. IRS employee Doug Edwards said that Mary Yate and Alice West have lunch together almost every day.
6. Frank Luther, Henry Allen's neighbor, said that Allen has no business running for city council when he can't even keep his dog in his own yard.
7. Felicia Dial said that she plans to vote for Henry Allen because he promises to run the city as efficiently as he runs his business.

8. IRS employee Mary Yate said that Frank Luther and Doug Edwards have been friends since grade school.

9. IRS employee Avery Page said that Alice West makes a lot of personal phone calls and once he heard her say, "He can't treat you like that!"

10. Henry Allen said that current council member Mavis Wright said that Susan Vickers said she'd do anything to win this election.

41. Which statement is most damaging to the Susan Vickers campaign?
    a. Statement 1
    b. Statement 3
    c. Statement 4
    d. Statement 10
    e. Statement 5

42. Which statement is least helpful to the investigation?
    a. Statement 1
    b. Statement 8
    c. Statement 2
    d. Statement 6
    e. Statement 4

43. Which two statements are hearsay?
    a. Statements 1 and 2
    b. Statements 9 and 10
    c. Statements 5 and 6
    d. Statements 3 and 4
    e. Statements 1 and 6

44. Which statement represents circumstantial evidence?
    a. Statement 5
    b. Statement 2
    c. Statement 4
    d. Statement 7
    e. Statement 3

45. Which statement indicates that an IRS employee is providing information to the Vickers campaign?
    a. Statement 1
    b. Statement 3
    c. Statement 10
    d. Statement 4
    e. Statement 8

46. Which two statements imply the possibility that the Allen campaign is attempting to make the Vickers campaign appear guilty?
    a. Statements 4 and 8
    b. Statements 1 and 3
    c. Statements 2 and 5
    d. Statements 8 and 10
    e. Statements 3 and 10

47. Which two statements tend to implicate Frank Luther?
    a. Statements 6 and 8
    b. Statements 1 and 5
    c. Statements 2 and 9
    d. Statements 4 and 5
    e. Statements 4 and 6

48. The police are staking out a suspected crack house. Officer Michaels is in front of the house. Officer Roth is in the alley behind the house. Officer Jensen is covering the windows on the north side, Officer Sheen those on the south. If Officer Michaels switches places with Officer Jensen, and Jensen then switches places with Officer Sheen, where is Officer Sheen?
    a. in the alley behind the house
    b. on the north side of the house
    c. in front of the house
    d. on the south side of the house

Use the following information to answer questions 49 and 50.

The first officer to respond to the scene of a sexual assault has many responsibilities. The officer should take the following steps in the order listed:

1. Aid the victim if necessary by calling for an ambulance or administering first aid.
2. Try to calm and comfort the victim as much as possible.
3. If the attack is recent, get a suspect description from the victim and radio the dispatcher to put out a be-on-the-lookout broadcast.
4. Find out from the victim where the crime occurred.
5. Determine whether there is any physical evidence on the victim that may need to be preserved, such as pieces of the suspect's skin or blood under the victim's fingernails.
6. If possible, have the victim change clothing, and then take the clothing he or she was wearing as evidence.
7. Convince the victim that he or she should undergo a medical exam for health and safety purposes, and so that evidence may be gathered.

49. At 2 A.M., Officer Maxwell is sent to the scene of a sexual assault at 1201 Roxy St. He arrives and finds the victim, Susan Jackson, sitting on the front porch crying. She tells him that a man crawled through her window and raped her. When the rapist ran out the front door, she called the police immediately. The next step Officer Maxwell should take is to
   a. take a look around the house to make sure the suspect is really gone.
   b. ask Jackson if she is injured and in need of medical attention.
   c. talk Jackson into going to the hospital for a medical exam.
   d. ask Jackson to describe her attacker.

50. Officer Augustine is at 2101 Reynolds Street talking to Betty Smith, the victim of a sexual assault. She is uninjured and is very calm. She gives Officer Augustine a detailed description of her attacker and says she thinks he may be headed for a nearby tavern. At this point, Officer Augustine should
   a. get into her patrol car and drive to the tavern.
   b. give the dispatcher the description of the suspect.
   c. take the victim straight to the hospital for a medical exam.
   d. have the victim change clothing.

Answers

1. a. If P.C. loses her U.S. citizenship without being denaturalized, then she must have expatriated. This question concerns a situation where there are two ways for naturalized U.S. citizens to lose U.S. citizenship, either by expatriation or by denaturalization. In choice **a**, the situation is considered in which P.C. has lost her U.S. citizenship without being denaturalized. Expatriation is the only option remaining to explain the loss of U.S. citizenship. Choices **b** and **e** are invalid because they fail to consider that there is more than one way for P.C. to lose U.S. citizenship. Choices **c** and **d** are about situations in which P.C. may or may not be denaturalized. These two choices are invalid because they fail to consider that there are several possible reasons for denaturalization.

2. b. No one ineligible to apply for permanent resident status was a national of Vietnam who was paroled into the United States through the Orderly Departure Program. This paragraph is mainly about the group of Vietnamese nationals who were paroled into the United States under the Orderly Departure Program with indefinite immigration status. In 2003, a new rule made everyone in this group of Vietnamese nationals (and some others) eligible to apply for permanent resident status. Accordingly, anyone who is not eligible to apply for permanent resident status must not be part of this group of Vietnamese nationals, which is equivalent to choice **b**. Choices **a** and **c** fail to recognize that others, such as nationals of Cambodia, were also eligible to apply for permanent resident status. Choices **d** and **e** contradict the information that everyone in the group of Vietnamese nationals who were paroled into the United States under the Orderly Departure Program was eligible to apply for permanent resident status.

3. c. If an applicant's documentation appears to be true and relevant to an employer, the employer must refuse acceptance and ask for other documentation from the government's list of acceptable documents. This question asks for the response option that CANNOT be validly concluded from the information in the paragraph. The only response option that cannot be validly concluded is choice **c.** Choice **c** is invalid because the paragraph does not say that employers must refuse acceptance of documentation that appears to be true and relevant. Choices **b** and **e** are valid based on the information in the first sentence. Choice **a** is valid based on the information in the second sentence that employers cannot change documentation requirements. Choice **d** is valid based on the information in the last sentence stating that employers may request different documentation when they believe the documentation submitted appears to be altered.

4. e. Only sector canine handlers have the authority to issue citations for misdemeanor marijuana and paraphernalia offenses committed in their presence. This question is a negative lead item, so the correct response is the only response option that CANNOT be validly concluded. The first sentence states that all state peace officers have authority to issue certain drug related citations. Choice **e** is invalid because it says that only sector canine handlers have such authority. The first sentence states that all state peace officers have authority to issue certain drug-related citations; therefore, at least some who have authority to issue certain drug-related citations must be peace officers, choice **a.** The last sentence states that all sector canine handlers are state peace officers; therefore, all sector canine handlers have authority to issue certain drug-related citations because the handlers are state peace officers, choice **b.** Moreover, given that all sector canine handlers have authority to issue certain drug-related citations, it must be the case that at least some individuals who have authority to issue certain drug-related citations are sector canine handlers, choice **c.** Finally, given that all sector canine handlers have authority to issue certain drug related citations, it must be the case that no sector canine handlers lack authority to issue certain drug related citations, choice **d.**

5. c. Green cards are the only work authorization documents that expire after ten years. This is a negative lead question, so the correct response is the only response option that cannot be validly concluded. Choice **c** is invalid because it assumes from the information that green cards are the *only* work authorization documents that expire after ten years. The fourth sentence states that all green card applicants must apply in person; therefore, an application that does not require applicants to apply in person cannot be a green card application, choice **a**. Choice **b** is valid and is based on the information in the third sentence. The second sentence establishes that green cards have an expiration date, so choice **d** is valid. The last sentence says that sometimes it takes a year to receive a new green card, so choice **e** is valid.

6. a. A person who is depressed is far more likely to commit suicide than someone who is simply not hungry, someone who is arguing, or someone who has been injured and finds it difficult to communicate because of the injury.

7. b. The officers have accomplished steps 1 and 2. Step 3 is to listen at the door.

8. d. Standing to one side of the door before knocking is the next step in the procedure after listening at the door.

9. c. The first step is for the officers to tell the dispatcher they have arrived at the scene.

10. a. The woman is bleeding and needs first aid. Choice **b** is not an option in the list of procedures. There aren't two people to separate as suggested in choice **c**. The woman knows he is a police officer, so there is no need to identify himself as suggested in choice **d**.

11. a. The speaker is committing the *ad hominem* fallacy. The speaker is discrediting the potential employee based on his beliefs, not on what he is capable of contributing. The correct answer is choice **a**.

12. c. After all the switching was done, Officer Jenkins was directly behind the suspect. Officer Burton had fallen and Officer Calvin turned back to help him. Officer Zeller remained in the rear.

13. c. The suspect described in Robbery #2 has a crew-cut hair style, is at least five inches taller than the other suspects, and is about 60 pounds heavier. The other three descriptions are much more likely to be of the same man because they all describe a similar build and mention one earring or a pierced ear.

14. a. The witnesses seem to agree that the plate starts out with the letter J. Three witnesses agree that the plate ends with 12L. Three witnesses think that the second letter is X, and a different three think that the third letter is K. The plate description that has all these common elements is choice **a**.

15. b. Dark green and gray roof are the elements repeated most often by the eyewitnesses and are therefore most likely correct.

16. b. The essential information from which the answer can be derived is contained in the third and fifth sentences. The third sentence tells us that some substances found at a crime scene yield valuable clues under microscopic examination. The fifth sentence explains that all substances found at a crime scene are potential sources of evidence. Therefore, choice **b** can be validly concluded. Choices **a**, **d**, and **e** are incorrect because they are not supported by the passage.

17. b. Choices **a**, **c**, **d**, and **e**, while they relate to issues discussed in the paragraph, draw conclusions that are not supported by the information given.

18. b. The paragraph makes it clear that communication skills are important for all border patrol agents. The word *only* makes choice **a** incorrect. Choices **c** and **e** are refuted by the paragraph. Choice **d** is not supported by the paragraph.

19. e. We know from the third sentence that the Type A micro pattern exists in 70% of all Acme Model 200 printers and in some other models of printers. However, we know neither how many other models nor what percentage of other models produce the Type A micro pattern. Accordingly, the probability that the note was printed on the Acme Model 200 printer cannot be determined. Consequently, choices **a**, **b**, **c**, and **d** are incorrect.

20. b. A specific rule contained in the procedures requires Agent Maguire to accompany the man to the hospital because the man refused to identify himself and was therefore unidentified.

21. c. Choice **c** is correct because the paragraph states that agricultural jobs are excluded from the seasonal visa program. The statements made in answers **a**, **b**, **d**, and **e** are refuted by the paragraph.

22. a. Choice **a** is supported by the information in the paragraph. Choice **b** is refuted by the paragraph. Choice **c** is refuted by the phrase *One way* in the first sentence. Choice **d** is not supported; no judgment is made in the paragraph about which way is best. Choice **e** is refuted by the facts in the paragraph.

23. c. The conclusions drawn by choices **a**, **b**, **d**, and **e** are refuted by the qualifications for naturalization outlined in the paragraph. Only choice **c** is a valid conclusion.

24. b. The passage speaks of two categories of deportable aliens, those who can be deported for committing prohibited acts before coming to the United States and those who can be deported for committing them since; therefore, logically, the alien need not have committed deportable offenses before entering the United States in order to be deported (supporting choice **b** and ruling out choices **a** and **c**). Choices **d** and **e** are examples—the word *only* at the beginning of each choice rules them out.

25. b. The passage states that an alien does not have *the right to hold federal elective office*; it does not speak about other types of office (supporting choice **b**). The other choices are affirmed in the passage and are therefore the wrong answers to this question.

26. b. Choice **b** is correct because the ability to work alone is stated in the paragraph, and the ability to think fast is implied by the complications of the job listed throughout the paragraph. The conclusions drawn by choices **a**, **c**, **d**, and **e** are refuted by the paragraph.

27. d. This conclusion is correct because the paragraph implies the importance of implementing several strategies at once. Each of the other choices incorrectly focuses on using one strategy at a time.

28. d. The conclusion drawn by choice **d** is supported by the content and tone of the quotes in the passage. Each of the conclusions offered in the other answers is refuted by the passage.

29. d. The passage says that A-3 visas *may be extended in increments* [regular additions] *of not more than two years*. Since the plural word (*increments*) is used, it is reasonable to assume more than one increment can be added (supporting choice **d** and ruling out choices **a** and **b**). Choice **c** applies to A-1 and A-2 visa holders. Choice **e** is not mentioned in the passage.

30. a. Choice **a** is a convoluted way of saying, in the negative, that Ron is guilty of entrapment if Sheryl were not intending to commit the crime until he suggested it. Choice **b** is incorrect because it says that Sheryl was already contemplating committing the crime. Choices **c**, **d**, and **e** contradict the passage by saying that (1) there was no entrapment, and (2) Sheryl would not have committed the crime unless Ron suggested it or led her to think it was legal.

31. b. If choice **b** is reworded to clear out unnecessary negatives, it will read *expatriation takes place only if the act of expatriating is voluntary*; therefore, choice **b** is correct. Choice **a** says denaturalization does not take place if the naturalization order was obtained illegally, which is incorrect. Choice **c** is fairly clear and is incorrect, since expatriation must be a voluntary act. Choices **d** and **e** are incorrect—little words like *unless* are very important.

32. b. Seeing a teenager with a spray paint can is the most suspicious of the incidents described since Officer Yang is looking for graffiti artists. Spray paint is not an item most people carry around with them, and is suspicious given the circumstances.

33. c. Choice **c** *is* an example of shoplifting because Gail made no attempt to pay for the cologne before leaving the business. Choice **a** is not an example of shoplifting because the clerk told Terry he did not have to pay for the candy. Terry did not hide the candy or try to leave the business without an attempt to pay. The clerk had the option of having Terry put back the candy, but he instead chose to give it away. Choice **b** is not an example of shoplifting because Gloria did not pass the last point of opportunity to pay before leaving the store without making an attempt to pay for the batteries. In businesses where the checkout stands are located in the middle or toward the rear of the store, the benefit of the doubt goes to the shopper until he or she walks out the door. Choice **d** is not an example of shoplifting because Abby paid for her son's candy, even though he ate the candy in the store and eventually walked out of the store.

34. c. Choice **a** is not a strong choice because a person's reputation has more to do with criminal history, or lack thereof, than his or her standing in the community. Moreover, if the city councilperson were warned about drunk driving, there is nothing to indicate that he or she would not continue the behavior. Both the known heroin addict and the woman on probation have reputations, like a criminal history, that run counter to giving warnings.

35. c. Of all the situations, only the case of the felony crime clearly prohibits the issuance of a warning.

36. b. Generally, stealing over $500 (choice **a**) and most frauds (choice **d**) are felony crimes.

37. c. Assault is the most serious crime, followed by, in descending order, burglary, breaking and entering, and extortion.

38. c. The officer has already performed step 1 by making sure the handcuffs are secure. Checking the suspect's waistband and back pocket area is step 2, which she should perform next. She should not be distracted by the bulge in the cap, so choice **b** is not correct.

39. a. The officer should check the arrestee's hat because that is the next step after checking the waistband and back pocket area. The officer should not be distracted from the proper procedures because the intoxicated man is difficult to control. The other officers are there to assist, and he should be able to safely conduct his search.

40. b. The officer should check the waistband area and the area near the arrestee's hands, because that is the next step on the list of procedures. That the arrestee is a woman and is wearing a dress should not distract the officer from following procedure, since dresses may have pockets and waistbands.

41. c. Statement 4 provides information on the opportunity the Vickers campaign had to receive information from the IRS.

42. d. Statement 6 is not related to the investigation at all.

43. b. Statements 9 and 10 are statements made without personal knowledge, simply repeating what others said.

44. a. Circumstantial evidence is evidence from which the presence of a principal fact of the case can be inferred. The fact that Mary Yate and Alice West frequently have lunch together by itself proves nothing; however, one may infer that it means they have a close relationship.

45. d. Statement 4 provides the opportunity for the campaign to receive information from the IRS.

46. c. Statements 2 and 5 indicate a connection from the Allen campaign to the IRS and then to the Vickers campaign.

47. a. Statements 6 and 8 show that Luther holds a grudge against Allen and has access to the IRS through Doug Edwards.

48. c. After all the switches are made, Officer Sheen is in front of the house. Officer Roth is in the alley behind the house; Officer Michaels is on the north side; and Officer Jensen is on the south.

49. b. Getting medical attention for the victim is the first step on the list of procedures. Choice **a** is not on the list of procedures, choice **c** is the last step on the list, and choice **d**, while important, is less urgent than determining whether Jackson is injured.

50. b. The officer has already taken care of steps 1 and 2: The victim doesn't need immediate medical help, and she is calm. Step 3 tells the officer to radio the suspect description to the dispatcher so a be-on-the-lookout bulletin can be issued.

PUTTING IT ALL TOGETHER

Congratulations!

You've completed all 21 lessons in *Reasoning Skills for Law Enforcement Exams*. At this point, you should have seen your critical thinking and reasoning skills improve greatly. By devoting the time that you did to consciously working on your reasoning skills, you have also improved your chances of scoring well on the law enforcement entrance exam of your choice. The time that you have remaining until you take the entrance exam should be spent reviewing some of the key lessons in this book and increasing your comfort with the various types of critical thinking/logical reasoning questions. To assist with this, the final lesson is devoted to reviewing the critical thinking and logical reasoning sections on various law enforcement entrance exams.

22 ▶ Critical Thinking/Logical Reasoning and Law Enforcement Exams

LESSON SUMMARY

Just about every law enforcement entrance exam will contain a critical thinking or a logical reasoning section. This chapter discusses those portions of the exams for border patrol agents, federal agents, treasury enforcement agents, corrections officers, police officers, deputy sheriffs, state police, police sergeants, and probation and parole officers.

About the Exams

As you will see, the structure and format of the critical thinking/logical reasoning sections on law enforcement exams are as varied as the jobs themselves. The reason for this is that each career develops its own entrance exam. Therefore, the police officer exam may contain more critical thinking/logical reasoning questions than the corrections officer exam and less than the federal agent exam. In addition to this, each exam has a different name for the critical thinking/logical reasoning section. What is important for you to remember is that whether

CRITICAL THINKING/LOGICAL REASONING AND LAW ENFORCEMENT EXAMS

the section is called Logical Reasoning, Situational Judgment, or simply Problem Solving, the skills needed to think through these questions and arrive at the correct answer are all the same—critical thinking and logical reasoning skills. These are the skills that form the backbone of this book.

Border Patrol Agent Exam

The critical thinking/logical reasoning section of the border patrol exam is found in the Logical Reasoning section. This section tests your ability to read, understand, and apply critical thinking skills as represented by real-life scenarios. There are 30 questions on this part of the exam. The questions are multiple choice with five possible answers from which to choose. The questions assess several key intellectual capabilities that are required of border patrol agents including problem solving and critical thinking. The questions in this section of the test are different from regular reading comprehension questions that ask you to understand the meaning of a passage. Specifically, this is the kind of reading that will test your ability to draw conclusions and take action. Often, the situations presented in the questions can be quite complex. Examples include:

- determining whether someone can be deported, based on different laws passed at different times
- determining whether someone who wishes to enter (or who has entered) the United States is entitled to refugee status or asylum status
- assessing valid reasons, based on provided regulations and laws, for someone to apply for refugee status from his or her home country

These examples may seem familiar to you, as you have answered quite a few logical reasoning questions based on the Logical Reasoning section of the border patrol agent exam.

Federal Agent Exam/ Treasury Enforcement Agent

The federal agent exam contains a section called Verbal Reasoning. Obviously, this is where you will find the critical thinking/logical reasoning questions on this exam. There are 30 questions in this section. The questions are in multiple-choice format with five answer choices. These questions are designed to assess several key intellectual capabilities that are required for you to succeed as a federal agent, including vocabulary, reading comprehension, and critical thinking skills. Often, the situations presented in the questions can be quite complex. Careful reading and focused thinking are required to determine what *is* being asked and what *is not* being asked. Keep in mind that, fortunately, the questions test *only* your understanding of the facts presented in each question, and you do *not* need to know any other information beyond what is presented to you. The questions simply test your ability to understand the information you read and to draw a logical conclusion from those facts. Examples include:

- determining whether an officer followed correct policy/procedure
- determining the evidentiary value of different articles of evidence

These examples may seem familiar to you as you have answered quite a few logical reasoning questions based on the Investigative/Verbal Reasoning section of the corrections officer exam.

Corrections Officer Exam

The critical thinking/logical reason section of corrections officer exams will vary depending upon the type of agency that you are testing for (federal, state, county, or municipal). For instance, the name of the section and the number of questions may differ depending on which exam you take. What will not vary are the skills that are being tested. The majority of corrections officer exams place critical thinking questions under the heading Situational Judgment/Reasoning. Situational Judgment/Reasoning questions ask you to climb inside the mind of a corrections officer and make decisions from that viewpoint. It is not necessary for you to know the laws of any state or the policies and procedures of any prison system. The test itself will give you all the information you need to answer the question. You will be tested, however, on your problem-solving skills and your ability to apply common sense and good judgment within the prison environment. This section usually consists of approximately 25 multiple-choice questions designed to see whether you can make a sound decision based on the information given to you. To arrive at the right conclusion, you need to apply common sense, good judgment, and good reading skills. Most of the questions focus on your ability to maintain security and order, the two most important components of a CO's job. Examples include:

- determining the proper course of action when dealing with an unruly prisoner
- assessing the actions of correction officers in their interactions with prisoners

These examples may seem familiar to you, as you have answered quite a few logical reasoning questions based on the Situational Judgment/Reasoning section of the corrections officer exam.

Police Officer/ Deputy Sheriff/ State Police/Police Sergeant

The critical thinking/logical reasoning section of the police officer exam is usually called Situational Judgment. On the deputy sheriff's exam it is simply called Judgment and on the state police exam it is called Problem Solving. On all three exams, the questions come in two basic varieties—deciding what course of action a fictional officer should take and drawing conclusions for eyewitness testimony. Situational judgment questions ask you to climb inside the mind of a police officer and make decisions from this viewpoint. It isn't necessary for you to know the laws of any state or the policies and procedures of any law enforcement agency. The test itself will give you the information you need to answer the question. Some exams put you right into the hot seat with language such as, "You are on patrol in a high-crime area" while other exams use a more subtle approach: "Officer Jones is on patrol when she sees a man breaking into a car." Although the approach is different, both test makers are asking you to look at their questions from the same viewpoint—a police officer's view. The structure of situational judgment questions is quite simple. You will be given a situation, and then you will be asked to choose how you would handle the situation if you were the police officer responding to that call. The nice part is that you don't have to come up with your own plan. You get to choose the best answer from four multiple-choice options that follow the question. These examples may seem familiar to you, as you have answered quite a few logical reasoning questions based upon the Situational Judgment/Reasoning section of the these exams.

Some police agencies now use one or more situational video exams called the Behavioral Personnel Assessment Device (B-PAD) to assess your judgment and interpersonal skills. If you are required to take a video exam in addition to or in place of a written exam, the same basic steps apply: Remember the importance of safety, use an appropriate amount of force, and take a common-sense approach. During a B-PAD exam, you will be shown eight short situations that are typical in a police officer's line of duty. For example, you may be asked to defuse hostile domestic disputes, calm an angry motorist, or comfort a lost child. You will most likely see one-on-one situations and group problems with a mixture of ethnic groups and ages. After each one- or two-minute situation is shown, you will have 45 seconds to respond to the actors in the video as if you were the officer handling the situation. Your response will be taped on a video camera, which is normally positioned right next to the video monitor. You will probably get to respond to a practice scene before beginning the actual test. The entire B-PAD takes about 20 minutes to complete. You will not be scored on your knowledge of any policies, procedures, or law. Rather, you will be assessed for your judgment, problem-solving, and interpersonal skills in dealing with different types of people in different situations commonly found in police work.

Probation/Parole Officer

The critical thinking/logical reasoning section on the probation officer/parole officer exam is usually called Investigative Concepts, or simply Concepts. This section utilizes case examples/scenarios to measure a candidate's ability to logically think through an actual probation violation case. The answers are in the form of multiple-choice and true/false questions. The test itself will give you all the information you need to answer the question. You will be tested, however, on your problem-solving skills and your ability to apply policy and good judgment within the probation and parole setting. The body of the question will contain all the necessary information; the true test is in the application.

APPENDIX
How to Prepare
for a Test ▶

Most of us get nervous about tests, especially career entrance tests, where our scores can have a significant impact on our future. Nervousness is natural—and it can even be an advantage if you know how to channel it into positive energy.

The following pages provide suggestions for overcoming test anxiety both in the days and weeks before the test and during the test itself.

Two to Three Months
before the Test

The number one best way to combat test anxiety is to **be prepared.** That means two things: Know what to expect on the test and review the material and skills on which you will be tested.

Know What to Expect

What knowledge or skills will the exam test? What are you expected to know? What skills will you be expected to demonstrate? What is the format of the test? Multiple choice? True or false? Essay? If possible, go to a bookstore or to the library and get a study guide that shows you what a sample test looks like. Or maybe the agency that's testing you for a job gives out a study guide or conducts study sessions. The fewer surprises you have on test day, the better you will perform. The more you know what to expect, the more confident you will be to handle the questions.

Review the Material and Skills You'll Be Tested On

The fact that you are reading this book means that you've already taken this step in regard to logic and reasoning questions. Now, are there other steps you can take? Are there other subject areas that you need to review? Can you make more improvement in this or other areas? If you are really nervous or if it has been a long time since you reviewed these subjects and skills, you may want to buy another study guide, sign up for a class in your neighborhood, or work with a tutor.

The more you know about what to expect on test day and the more comfortable you are with the material and skills to be tested, the less anxious you will be and the better you will do on the test itself.

The Days before the Test

Review, Don't Cram

If you have been preparing and reviewing in the weeks before the exam, there's no need to cram a few days before the exam. Cramming is likely to confuse you and make you nervous. Instead, schedule a relaxed review of all that you have learned.

Physical Activity

Get some exercise in the days preceding the test. You'll send some extra oxygen to your brain and allow your thinking performance to peak on the day you take the test. Moderation is the key here. You don't want to exercise so much that you feel exhausted, but a little physical activity will invigorate your body and brain. Walking is a terrific, low-impact, energy-building form of exercise.

Balanced Diet

Like your body, your brain needs the proper nutrients to function well. Eat plenty of fruits and vegetables in the days before the test. Foods high in lecithin, such as fish and beans, are especially good choices. Lecithin is a protein your brain needs for peak performance. You may even consider a visit to your local pharmacy to buy a bottle of lecithin tablets several weeks before your test.

Rest

Get plenty of sleep the nights before you take the test. Don't overdo it, though, or you'll make yourself as groggy as if you were overtired. Go to bed at a reasonable time, early enough to get the number of hours you need to function **effectively**. You'll feel relaxed and rested if you've gotten plenty of sleep in the days before you take the test.

Trial Run

At some point before you take the test, make a trial run to the testing center to see how long it takes you to get there. Rushing raises your emotional energy and lowers your intellectual capacity, so you want to allow plenty of time on test day to get to the testing center. Arriving ten or fifteen minutes early gives you time to relax and get situated.

Motivation

Plan some sort of celebration—with family or friends, or just by yourself—for after the test. Make sure it's something you'll really look forward to and enjoy. If you have something to look forward to after the test is over, you may find it easier to prepare and keep moving during the test.

Test Day

It's finally here, the day of the big test. Set your alarm early enough to allow plenty of time to get to the testing center. Eat a good breakfast. Avoid anything that's really high in sugar, such as doughnuts. A sugar high turns into a sugar low after an hour or so. Cereal, toast, or anything with complex carbohydrates is a good choice. Eat only moderate amounts. You don't want to take a test feeling stuffed! Your body will channel its energy to your digestive system instead of your brain.

Pack a high-energy snack to take with you. You may have a break sometime during the test when you can grab a quick snack. Bananas are great. They have a moderate amount of sugar and plenty of brain nutrients, such as potassium. Most proctors won't allow you to eat a snack while you're testing, but a peppermint shouldn't pose a problem. Peppermints are like smelling salts for your brain. If you lose your concentration or suffer from a momentary mental block, a peppermint can get you back on track. Don't forget the earlier advice about relaxing and taking a few deep breaths.

Leave early enough so you have plenty of time to get to the test center. Allow a few minutes for unexpected traffic. When you arrive, locate the restroom and use it. Few things interfere with concentration as much as a full bladder. Then find your seat and make sure it's comfortable. If it isn't, tell the proctor and ask to move to something you find more suitable.

Now relax and think positively! Before you know it, the test will be over, and you'll walk away knowing you've done as well as you can.

Combating Test Anxiety

Okay—you know what the test will be on. You've reviewed the subjects and practiced the skills on which you will be tested. So why do you still have that sinking feeling in your stomach? Why are your palms sweaty and your hands shaking?

Even the brightest, most well-prepared test takers sometimes suffer bouts of test anxiety. But don't worry; you can overcome it. Here are some specific strategies to help you.

Take the Test One Question at a Time

Focus all your attention on the one question you're answering. Block out any thoughts about questions you've already read or concerns about what's coming next. Concentrate your thinking where it will do the most good—on the question you're answering now.

Develop a Positive Attitude

Keep reminding yourself that you're prepared. In fact, if you've read this book or any other in the Learning-Express Skill Builder series, you're probably better prepared than most other test takers. Remember, it's only a test, and you're going to do your **best**. That's all anyone can ask of you. If that nagging drill sergeant voice inside your head starts sending negative messages, combat them with positive ones of your own. Tell yourself:

- "I'm doing just fine."
- "I've prepared for this test."
- "I know exactly what to do."
- "I know I can get the score I'm shooting for."

You get the idea. Remember to drown out negative messages with positive ones of your own.

If You Lose Your Concentration

Don't worry about it! It's normal. During a long test, it happens to everyone. When your mind is stressed or overexerted, it takes a break whether you want it to or not. It's easy to get your concentration back if you simply acknowledge the fact that you've lost it and take a quick break. Your brain needs very little time (seconds, really) to rest.

Put your pencil down and close your eyes. Take a deep breath, hold it for a moment, and let it out slowly. Listen to the sound of your breathing and repeat this two more times. The few seconds this takes is really all the time your brain needs to relax and get ready to refocus. This exercise also helps control your heart rate, so that you can keep anxiety at bay.

Try this technique several times when you feel stressed in the days before the test. The more you practice, the better it will work for you on test day.

If You Freeze

Don't worry about a question that stumps you even though you're sure you know the answer. Mark it and go on to the next question. You can come back to the stumper later. Try to put it out of your mind completely until you come back to it. Just let your subconscious mind chew on the question while your conscious mind focuses on the other items (one at a time, of course). Chances are, the memory block will be gone by the time you return to the question.

If you freeze before you even begin the test, here's what to do:

- Do some deep breathing to help yourself relax and focus.
- Remind yourself that you're prepared.
- Take a little time to look over the test.
- Read a few of the questions.
- Decide which ones are the easiest and start there.

Before long, you'll be in the groove.

Time Strategies

One of the most important—and nerve-wracking—elements of a standardized test is time. You'll only be allowed a certain number of minutes for each section, so it is very important that you use your time wisely.

Pace Yourself

The most important time strategy is **pacing yourself**. Before you begin, take just a few seconds to sur-vey the test, making note of the number of questions and of the sections that look easier than the rest. Then, make a rough time schedule based on the amount of time available to you. Mark the halfway point on your test and make a note beside that mark of what the time will be when the testing period is half over.

Keep Moving

Once you begin the test, **keep moving**. If you work slowly in an attempt to make fewer mistakes, your mind will become bored and begin to wander. You'll end up making far more mistakes if you're not concentrating. Worse, if you take too long to answer questions that stump you, you may end up running out of time before you finish.

Don't stop for difficult questions. Skip them and move on. You can come back to them later if you have time. A question that takes you five seconds to answer counts as much as one that takes you several minutes, so pick up the easy points first. Besides, answering the easier questions first helps build your confidence and gets you in the testing groove. Who knows? As you go through the test, you may even stumble across some relevant information to help you answer those tough questions.

Don't Rush

Keep moving, but **don't rush.** Think of your mind as a seesaw. On one side is your emotional energy. On the other side is your intellectual energy. When your emotional energy is high, your intellectual capacity is low. Remember how difficult it is to reason with someone when you're angry? Alternately, when your intellectual energy is high, your emotional energy is low. Rushing raises your emotional energy and reduces your intellectual capacity. Remember the last time you were late for work? All that rushing around probably caused you to forget important things—like your lunch. Move quickly to keep your mind from wandering, but don't rush and get yourself flustered.

Check Yourself

Check yourself at the halfway mark. If you're a little ahead, you know you're on track and may even have a little time left to check your work. If you're a little behind, you have several choices. You can pick up the pace a little, but do this *only* if you can do it comfortably. Remember—**don't rush!** You can also skip around in the remaining portion of the test to pick up as many easy points as possible. This strategy has one drawback, however. If you are marking a bubble-style answer sheet and you put the right answers in the wrong bubbles—they're wrong. So pay close attention to the question numbers if you decide to do this.

Avoiding Errors

When you take the test, you want to make as few errors as possible in the questions you answer. Here are a few tactics to keep in mind.

Control Yourself

Remember that comparison between your mind and a seesaw? Keeping your emotional energy low and your intellectual energy high is the best way to avoid mistakes. If you feel stressed or worried, stop for a few seconds. Acknowledge the feeling (Hmmm! I'm feeling a little pressure here!), take a few deep breaths, and send yourself some positive messages. This relieves your emotional anxiety and boosts your intellectual capacity.

Directions

In many standardized testing situations, a proctor reads the instructions aloud. Make certain you understand what is expected. If you don't, **ask.** Listen carefully for instructions about how to answer the questions and make certain you know how much time you have to complete the task. Write the time on your test if you don't already know how long you have to take the test. If you miss this vital information, **ask for it.** You need it to do well on your test.

Answers

This may seem like a silly warning, but it is important. Place your answers in the right blanks or the corresponding ovals on the answer sheet. Right answers in the wrong place earn no points—they may even lose points. It's a good idea to check every five to ten questions to make sure you're in the right spot. That way, you won't need much time to correct your answer sheet if you have made an error.

Logic and Judgment Questions

Standardized tests often feature a section designed to test your judgment, common sense, or logic. Often, these questions are based on a hypothetical situation, which may be presented in a separate paragraph or as part of the question. Here are a few tactics for approaching such questions.

This may seem strange, but a few questions can be answered without reading the passage. If the passage is short (four sentences or so), read the questions first. You may be able to answer them by using your common sense. You can check your answers later after you've actually read the passage. If you're unsure, though, *don't guess;* read the passage carefully. If you can't answer any of the questions, you still know what to look for in the passage. This focuses your reading and makes it easier for you to retain important information. If you know what to look for ahead of time, it's easier to find the information.

Questions based on a hypothetical situation actually test your reading ability as much as your logic and common sense. So be sure you read the situation carefully. **Circle** information that tells who, what, when, or where. The circles will be easy to locate later if you come across a question that asks for specific information. Marking up a passage in this way also heightens your concentration and makes it more likely that you'll remember the information when you answer the questions following the passage. Be sure to read the questions and answer choices carefully, too. A simple word like *not* can turn a right answer into a wrong answer.

Choosing the Right Answers by Process of Elimination

Make sure you understand what the question is asking. If you're not sure of what's being asked, you'll never know whether you've chosen the right answer. So figure out what the question is asking. If the answer isn't readily apparent, look for clues in the answer choices. Notice the similarities and differences in the answer choices. Sometimes, this helps put the question in a new perspective and makes it easier to answer. If you're still not sure of the answer, use the process of elimination. First, eliminate any answer choices that are obviously wrong. Then, reason your way through the remaining choices. You may be able to use relevant information from other parts of the test. If you can't eliminate any of the answer choices, it might be better to skip the question and come back to it later. If you can't eliminate any answer choices to improve your odds when you come back later, then make a guess and move on.

If You're Penalized for Wrong Answers

You **must know** whether there's a penalty for wrong answers before you begin the test. If you don't, ask the proctor before the test begins. Whether you make a guess depends on the penalty. Some standardized tests are scored in such a way that every wrong answer reduces your score by one-fourth or one-half of a point. Whatever the penalty, if you can eliminate enough choices to make the odds of answering the question better than the penalty for getting it wrong, make a guess.

Let's imagine you are taking a test in which each answer has four choices and you are penalized one-fourth of a point for each wrong answer. If you have no clue and cannot eliminate any of the answer choices, you're better off leaving the question blank because the odds of answering correctly are one in four. This makes the penalty and the odds equal. However, if you can eliminate one of the choices, the odds are now in your favor. You have a one in three chance of answering the question correctly. Fortunately, few tests are scored using such elaborate means, but if your test is one of them, know the penalties and calculate your odds before you take a guess on a question.

If You Finish Early

Use any time you have left at the end of the test or test section to check your work. First, make certain you've put the answers in the right places. As you're doing this, make sure you've answered each question only once. Most standardized tests are scored in such a way that questions with more than one answer are marked wrong. If you've erased an answer, make sure you've done a good job. Check for stray marks on your answer sheet that could distort your score.

After you've checked for these obvious errors, take a second look at the more difficult questions. You've probably heard the folk wisdom about never changing an answer. It's not always good advice. If you have a good reason for thinking a response is wrong, change it.

After the Test

Once you've finished, *congratulate yourself.* You've worked hard to prepare; now it's time to enjoy yourself and relax. Remember that celebration you planned before the test? Now it's time to go to it!